W9-APH-810

The New Job Search

Break All The Rules.
Get Connected.
And Get Hired Faster
For The Money You're Worth

By

Molly Wendell

www.mollywendell.com

Molly Wendell

Copyright © 2009

Molly Wendell

North Audley Media

USA

All Rights Reserved. Printed in the United States of America. Except as permitted under the United States Copyright Act of 1976, no part of this publication can be reproduced or distributed in any form or by any means, or stored in databases or retrieval systems, without the prior written permission of the publisher.

This book includes information that is published for general reference and is not intended to be a substitute for independent verification by readers when necessary and appropriate. The book is sold with the understanding that neither the author, editor nor publisher is engaged in rendering any legal, psychological or accounting advice. The publisher disclaims any personal liability, directly or indirectly, for advice or information presented within.

LCCN: 2009930661

ISBN: 978-0-9816432-4-3

This book is dedicated to everyone who has ever been or ever will be in a job search. Know that you're not alone. And there are many people who want to help you. They just may not know it yet.

Molly Wendell

TABLE OF CONTENTS

Molly Wendell

ACKNOWLEDGEMENTS

To the late Bob Schaninger for his wisdom in getting together a group of people in the job search – just to talk and share ideas. None of this would have been possible without him. Bob found out he had cancer the day after he landed a job. It kind of puts your job search in perspective. Bob passed away in 2005, but his legacy will live on forever.

To God whom I questioned repeatedly about why I had to be in a job search for so long. Who I came to know closer as a result of being in the job search for so long. And I came to realize that through His plan – I would be able to help far more people than just myself. It's all so clear now. But I'd tell you it certainly wasn't back then!

To Kevin Saunders, my Bible teacher, who gave me something to look forward to every Wednesday. Kevin, I don't know if you remember the day my mom put a prayer in the prayer offerings "Please pray that Molly gets a job soon." It made me sad (what didn't back then?). But, knowing that a couple hundred people were putting a word into God for me – now that made me happy!

To Jamie Glass for reminding me that sometimes you have to break your own self-imposed rules in order to truly be successful. We met during our respective job searches and have been great friends ever since. I can't imagine what my life would be like without her in it!

To Eileen Gibson for coming in at the final hour with a fresh set of eyes and ensuring what I was trying to say is what was actually said. I met Eileen's husband, Jim, at one of our meetings. He said "You two must meet." And, he was right!

To all of the members of Executives Network. Those who I've personally seen go through the job search – who eventually understand that there's a reason they're in it. And there will be a time when they won't be in it any longer. Thank you for all of your encouragement that gave me the motivation to continue helping others. And thank you for taking the time to help others who are going through what you went through. You are very much appreciated.

And to my family. Thank you for always being there. During the highs, the lows, and everything in between. Your love and support means absolutely everything to me.

INTRODUCTION

Getting laid off was the best thing that ever happened to me. Really.

If I hadn't been laid off, I probably would have been in the World Trade Center on the 102nd floor on September 11, 2001. So really. Getting laid off was the best thing that ever happened to me.

I was in the job search for two years and three days. And it wasn't easy.

About a year into my search, I got a job as a bartender at a sports bar. I had no experience. I had no idea what I was doing. How hard could it be? Turns out it was pretty easy. I wasn't the best at making mixed drinks, mostly because I could never remember what was in them. Unless you ordered something like Jack & Coke. That was a cinch! I remember someone ordering JB and Coke. I didn't know what JB was, so I just poured some type of amber-looking alcohol. It was only during inventory (which for some reason, I always got asked to do) that I learned Jim Beam was JB and I'd been serving the wrong drink to people for about six months. Oh well.

My first week as a bartender, a group of customers, mostly guys, came in. They were headed to the Arizona Diamondbacks baseball game and had an extra ticket for the swimming pool area. Did I want to go? My boss was standing right there, and said, "Absolutely, she'd love to!" Really, I would? Is that what this job entails? But, I thought, I've never been in that coveted area of Chase Field, so why not?

I got off work just after the game started and walked the couple blocks to the stadium. I went into the stadium – grabbed a beer – and made my way to the pool area. I showed the attendant my ticket and started walking down the steps. All of a sudden I heard, "Hey, here comes the bartender!" And that's when it hit me. That's my new identity. I'm a bartender. Never mind what I used to do. None of these people even knew that I spent many years in corporate America. All I am to them is a bartender. I held back the tears from my eyes, broke into a big smile, embraced my new identity and said, "Yes, here comes the bartender!"

Bartending wasn't the only job I took on. I had a mortgage to pay. I had bills. I had to generate cash. I worked as a photographer at golf courses; taking pictures of foursomes and selling them on a beautiful plaque customized with their picture that would be ready by the time they finished the round. And did they want to buy one? For every plaque I sold, I got $5. On a bad day, I walked away with $50. On a good day, $250.

Sometimes I'd work two tournaments a day. One weekend I generated $1,000 selling plaques. In this job, I was known as the photographer girl. I had to put up with lots of drunk people – doing their best to ruin the course. The reality is that I was probably more educated, had held higher-level positions, and could drive a golf ball much better than these people. But they were standing between me and my mortgage… so c'mon, please buy the plaque!

I paid my mortgage that year in cash. Most of it was in one dollar bills. The bank hated me. When they'd see me come in with my shopping bag, they knew whoever got stuck with me would get stuck counting out a couple thousand dollars. I was not popular there. I wanted to tell them I used to have direct deposit. I wanted to tell them I was not thrilled either that I had to pay my mortgage in singles. I wanted to tell them that this nightmare would end soon. But I didn't really know when it would end.

As it turned out, the nightmare would end, but that's only because I took a different approach. About 1 ½ years into my search, I decided something had to change. The economy was bad.

The dotcom bust had decimated opportunities for VPs of Marketing in Technology. I decided to try out a new industry. I had no experience and knew only two people in this industry. One I'd met during some work on a political campaign. The other I'd fought against in a zoning hearing about five years before. I called them up and asked for a meeting. The first one was easy. The second one, went something like this:

"Hi, it's Molly Wendell, remember me?"

"How could I forget you?"

"Great! I need your help! When can we meet?"

"How about Tuesday, 7 a.m. at Starbucks?"

"Perfect, see you then. Thank you!"

Within ninety days, I had 60 meetings and had more than 30 job offers… all for positions never posted… in an industry in which I had no experience.

I'm here to tell you there's a different way to approach your job search. And it's going to be exciting, and just a little bit scary. But open your mind to the possibility that it just might work. You might just find that you're having more fun, meeting more people and landing the job you want for the money you're worth!

Molly Wendell

The New Job Search

Break All The Rules.
Get Connected.
And Get Hired Faster
For The Money You're Worth

Molly Wendell

CHAPTER 1: DO YOU KNOW WHY YOU WERE PUT IN THIS JOB SEARCH?

I was out with some friends. One person, Joe, told me that he needed to get his knee replaced. Seeing that he didn't quite look like a card-carrying member of AARP, I asked him why. Running up mountains as fast as he can to get his heart rate close to 200. Marathons, triathlons, ultra runs, you name it. He's done it. Apparently, he's kind of an extremist – and that's an understatement! He just got a double hernia from weightlifting. Way to go, Joe!

He longs to get his knee replaced so he can take that 100 mile bike ride again, to run up the mountains, to hit the training circuit… hard!

And this got me thinking. How many people are so focused on being who they've always been that they forget to think about who they're supposed to be? Maybe Joe doesn't need to keep repeating past achievements. Maybe it's time for Joe to take his energies in another direction (before there is no Joe anymore!). Maybe this aching knee and double hernia are just signs that Joe needs to head down a new path? Is Joe reading the signs that are being put right in front of him? Maybe, but to him what says "Proceed with Caution" may really mean "Wrong Way."

How many other people are misinterpreting (or just plain ignoring) the signs right in front of them?

I see it happen all the time with people in their job searches. Craig, a CIO, has been doing the same thing for twenty years. One day Craig finds himself out of work, only to go right back to looking for the next CIO gig. He never even wanted to be a CIO. He longed to own a business. But he doesn't see that now is the time; it's the perfect time to figure it all out. Research what's out there. Buy that business. Maybe start his own. Instead of moving forward, Craig slams into reverse and presses the accelerator. It's no wonder he's miserable for twenty more years.

Are you ignoring the signs? Are you so focused on being who you've always been that you're forgetting to think about who you're supposed to be? Maybe there's a reason you were put in this job search. Maybe it's time for you to take your energies in another direction. Maybe it's time to throw away the rear-view mirror and focus forward. And see what possibilities might lie ahead.

Maybe it's time to realize that there's more to life than the life you've already lived. Even if you have to go through a few knees to get there. Right, Joe?!

Welcome to the Job Search

You're in transition... out of work... you've been made available. Whatever you want to call it, being in the job search is an incredible opportunity if you use it to your best advantage.

You've been given the gift of time to determine what you want to do with the rest of your life. Those who take the time, investigate options, and build new relationships come out of this transition not only more mentally grounded, but far more prepared for the next time they're in transition. Because, as we all know, there will be a next time.

Guess how many people want to hear your job search story? The one where you talk about the fact that you were laid off.... A while back, I was talking to four different people who were out of work. This was nothing unusual because my business is working with people who are unemployed. Two of them felt some pressing need to tell me in painstaking detail how they came to be in their current situations. The other two decided to share with me, yet again, an aspect of how great they were at their previous job and how others at the company couldn't believe they were let go.

I hate to tell you this. But I must. I've had enough! I've heard enough! Quit sharing your story with me. Quit sharing the story of how you were terminated, let go, laid off, fired, RIF'd, downsized... whatever you want to call it. Quit bringing up anything remotely related to the concept that you're no longer there. You know who wants to hear that story? No one. That's right. No one! Your family doesn't want to hear it... for the millionth time. Your friends don't want to hear it... for the thousandth time. And strangers don't want to hear it... for the first time. We get it. You're available.

Now, before you think I'm some unsympathetic, uncaring, downright mean person (it may be too late!)... let me explain.

Every time you bring up your story, you're bringing up the negative feelings associated with it.

No matter how much you say it doesn't matter... you sound bitter.

No matter how much you say you're glad you're not there anymore... you sound angry.

No matter how much you say you're better off... you come across sounding just a little bit insecure.

Maybe you're all of these. Maybe the company really did a number on you. Regardless of how it happened, you probably need to go through the stages of grief. And that's okay. You're not alone. Many others have been there before... and will go there again. Here are the common stages of grief you might be going through:

- Denial. "This isn't happening to me! I was the best employee. No one at the company could believe it."

3

- Anger. "Why is this happening to me? Someone needs to pay! I need to talk to an employment attorney."

- Bargaining. "I promise I'll (fill in the blank) if I could only land a job." (Lots of praying in this stage.)

- Depression. "I don't know if I'll ever find a job. I used to be a somebody."

- Acceptance. "I'm ready for whatever comes. I'm going to be okay. I had a great job before and I will again. It may take longer than I expected. I may have to get real creative when it comes to expenses. I may have to work a little harder at it, but the right position will come to me."

I'm not suggesting you go through this all alone. I'm simply recommending that you quit bringing up the negative feelings of the past.

Quit sharing your story with everyone you know. They feel bad for you. They have pity on you. They're scared to invite you to their party – because you may bring the whole party down.

Quit sharing your story with everyone you meet. You're making them uncomfortable! They don't know you from Adam… and all of a sudden you hit them with the biggest challenge you have in life today. Yikes! Why don't you ease into the relationship with something a little more positive (and less personal)?

Make a decision today that you're going to get over the past (or at least quit talking about it!). You're going to realize that you're not the first person to lose a job. And you certainly won't be the last. Make a decision that you'll go through the grief – but in the comfort and privacy of your own home. And then make a decision that today is the day your life will begin fresh.

4

You are meant for great things. You are destined for great opportunities. You're a fantastic, incredible person who has much to offer a company. You will find the right position. But not within the confines of your home. (Remember, that's where you left grief for the night!) You will find the right position by getting out there, meeting new people, and having interesting conversations. And when you do that, amazingly, the right opportunity is going to come knocking on your door. Answer it!

But before I tell you how to do it right, let's look at how you're doing it wrong!

You're Doing it Wrong!

I've watched people in the job search for more than seven years. And as the economy gets worse, so does their approach to finding and landing the next great opportunity. Here's what "You're Doing it Wrong" looks like:

1. **You focus on your resume.** You rework it until you've driven yourself crazy. Every person you ask has a different opinion of it. And just when you think you've got it perfect, someone comes along and tells you that it needs some serious revamping.

2. **You list yourself with the major job sites**. After you spent all that time working on your resume, you now spend hours upon hours uploading your resume content to the major job sites. But why? Do you honestly think they care? No. Now you're just on their mailing list. When was the last time you got called by someone because you were one of the hundreds of millions of people who have a listing?

3. **You spend valuable time surfing the job boards.**
Going through the job boards may make you feel like
you're working hard on your search. You review each
job posting and carefully select which ones you'd be
perfect for. You spend time thoughtfully composing a
well-worded cover email. Finally, you hit send. And then
you wait. And wait. And wait. Did you know that more
than 94 percent of companies never even respond to
candidates who apply for a position?

4. **You call every recruiter you know.** Don't get me
wrong, recruiters provide a valuable resource to
corporations by finding great candidates. It's just that
recruiters are paid for bringing in candidates that
EXACTLY match the company's criteria. Once the
position is put in the recruiter's hands, if you don't meet
12 out of the 10 attributes – yes, this includes the two
criteria they never even thought of – then you're
wasting their time. Recruiters don't typically have a lot
of time to spend with you if you're not a fit for what
they're working on today. It's the classic cold call
technique that went away (or at least should have!) in
the '80s: "Would you like to buy from me today? No,
okay, I'll call you back in ninety days."

5. **You send your resume to everyone you know telling
them you're looking for a job.** Hey, want a quicker
way to make people have pity on you? Guess what,
there isn't one. What you're really looking for is help.
But sending a generic email to everyone just makes
them feel sorry for you, and they don't know how to
help you – unless of course you end with the all-
important line: "If you know of any companies looking
for someone with my skills, please let me know."

Quit sending people your sad, pathetic email. If you really think you need to tell your circle about your job search via email – think again! If they're that close, they already know about you, and if they knew about an opportunity, they would have told you.

So let's get on with it. Your job search. And let's do it right this time. Let's take an approach that will position you for success... as infrequently as possible!

Molly's Takeaways

1. Don't waste precious time on the Internet when you could be talking with a real live person.
2. Remember, a recruiter will beat down your door if you're the perfect person for the job.
3. Focus forward. You've had a negative experience. That doesn't mean you should become a negative person.
4. You're going to find a fantastic opportunity. It may take longer than you think. It may take more work than you think. But you'll get there. And one day, you just might look back on this time and realize that you've become a better person because of it.

Molly Wendell

CHAPTER 2: THE BASICS

Everything you thought about job search is not true (or it is true… depending on whom you're listening to). Don't be so fixated on following what you perceive to be the rules of job search. Because, throughout this book, you're going to find out that the job search rules, as you know them today, are about to be broken. And you're going to be just the one to do it!

Job Search Rules Were Made to Be Broken

Recently, I was talking to Mark about a potential opportunity. A company had posted a position and then pulled it a couple of days later. I found out (serendipitously from some guy sitting next to me on an airplane) that the position was still viable, but they had some procedural things to deal with before re-posting it. I told Mark about it. He called my new airplane friend, and then told me that as soon as it was re-posted, he was going to apply. Why? Why wait? Why not network your way into the company before it ever gets posted? In fact, why don't you get to the hiring manager, get a meeting, have a conversation and save them from having to post it in the first place?

And then I wondered… Mark, why didn't you think of that? Why did you have to wait for a posting? Is that the rule? Who wrote these rules? And who says you have to follow them?

All this nonsense about rules got me thinking about a brain profiling tool I use called Emergenetics. Emergenetics helps you understand how people think. It divides the brain into four quadrants. The left side includes Analytical & Structural, the right Conceptual & Social/Relational. (If you want more details about how to use it in your job search, go to www.emergeneticsus.com.)

What I realized is that people who have a lot of structure in their brain (and by structure, I mean people who have a preference toward rules, guidelines, process, procedures) may find themselves stymied in today's job market. And here's why. People with a dominant tendency toward structure expect that everyone else will, of course, follow the same set of rules and guidelines that they believe should be in place.

And… the thing of it is, in today's job market, one of the most important things to do is forget the rules. I mean, it might benefit you to have a complete and utter disregard for any rules you believe might exist. After all, who made up the stupid rules anyway? Here are some of the rules that, in my opinion, you should make every effort to break:

1. **We only take applications online.** Let's say a CEO met the absolute perfect person for a VP-level position that wasn't even posted. You're telling me that the CEO would tell them they need to apply online! I don't think so. If you see a position online, and are really interested in it, get a contact within the company and have them introduce you to the hiring manager.

2. **I need to send my resume to people if they're going to help me with my job search.** No you don't! Who says so? Nobody, that's who! You don't need to send your resume to anyone. What you need to do is ask people for contacts and connections. And then you need to follow up on those and have actual real live conversations with people, without your past history (in the form of a resume) getting in the way.

   "But, they need to see my background." No they don't. Guess what. Nobody cares about your background. Nobody cares that you "Decreased costs by 15% while cutting staff by 30%." Half the time, we don't even understand the type of work you did. The other half, we're not really all that impressed with your so-called accomplishments. But the good news is that we know people. And we can connect you to people. But we're only going to connect you to people if you promise to quit waving your resume like a white flag in front of everyone's faces... and learn how to be a real live human being who's capable of having a real live, engaging conversation.

3. **They're laying off people so they must not be hiring.** You know what... while the company is getting rid of 20 percent of its workforce, the 80 percent who are still there are thinking, "I might be next. I'd better start looking." What's the company going to do when those people in key positions leave on their own accord? Well, they're going to replace them, that's what. While HR thinks their only issue is planned attrition, they now have a real challenge. Unplanned attrition. And do you think the hiring manager who was just left in the lurch is going to have the luxury of time and a long, drawn out hiring process? No, they need to get this person replaced as soon as possible, with minimal interruption to the business. You're the perfect person and you can start tomorrow. Great! You're hired!

4. **Just because they ask you a question doesn't mean you have to answer it.** Without being a downright liar (which I do not recommend at all!), there are ways to avoid answering a question you don't feel like answering. My favorite question to not answer is the age-old, "What are your weaknesses?" Usually what I want to say is, "My incredible lack of tolerance for people who come up with stupid questions like that. That's my weakness!" But I refrain... and turn that question into some really useful information for both of

us. I say, "Well, what I really don't enjoy is routine, maintenance type work. So if you're looking for someone to do the same thing every day, to implement a strategy that's already been planned, I'm definitely not your person. On the other hand, if you're looking for someone to figure out the strategy, to expand new markets, to build new businesses, and hire the team to get us there, that's where I excel and you'd be crazy not to have me on your team."

This type of answer accomplishes a couple of things. First, it tells them what makes me the wrong person for the job. Then, it tells them what makes me the right person for the job. Now, they can check off the box that I answered the question. Even though I really didn't. I answered a different question that was never even asked. So what? I'm doing them a favor by either taking me out of the hunt, or putting me at the front of the pack.

Perhaps my own complete lack of preference in the Structural side of the brain makes it easy for me to disregard the rules. I've always thought, "They certainly didn't mean me when they made up that rule. That line, oh that's for the people who like lines... not me." Try adopting that kind of mindset, at least while you're in the job search. Think about what everyone else is going to do... and then do the opposite.

Does the job fair begin at 9 a.m.? Show up at 7:30 a.m., go in the back entrance and get to know some people at your target company by helping set up their booth. Better yet, call the company putting on the event and offer to work the corporate registration table.

Does the website say apply online? Find someone who knows the hiring manager and get a meeting.

Does the person tell you to send them your resume? Tell them you'd love to... "but real quick, while I have you on the phone, let's set up a time to meet." And then bring the resume with you to the meeting – but don't ever give it to them. Instead, find out who they know and who else you can get connected to.

Forget other people's rules. Be your own boss! And make up your own rules! You might just find the process a lot more effective (and a little less frustrating).

Okay. Are you ready to start your search? To build a house, you need some plans and tools to ensure a solid foundation, the same goes for job search. Let's get the best possible foundation for your search by starting with a few basics.

These are relevant not only for the job search, but beyond. The basics consist of your Business Card, Email Address, The Handshake (and you probably already thought you knew how to do that!), and Being Prepared.

Your Business Card for the Job Search

When was the last time you received a letter? If you're like most people, it's been quite a while. I used to love checking my mailbox for letters. Now I'm lucky if I check it every two weeks. My postal carrier has become an expert at stuffing in as much mail as can fit (or not). Thanksgiving turkey… watch out!!

And if you're in the job search, the "thin envelope/rejection letter" doesn't even show up anymore. So why do people waste valuable space on the job search business card by putting on their mailing address? Here's where else job seekers go wrong in their quest to create the perfect job search business card.

1. **Too many designs.** It may be cute, and you may just LOVE sunflowers, but plant them in the ground, not on your card! A colorful design that encompasses the entire card makes it very difficult to read the type. On the

other hand, a completely boring, plain white card with black writing might need a little pizzazz.

2. **Multiple phone numbers.** I see many cards with a home (or home office) and a cell number. Here's what happens when you put two numbers on the card. First, they have to figure out which one to call. Then, when you don't answer that phone, they call you at the other phone. Chances are they'll leave a message at one of the numbers (hopefully not both). Either way, it's a waste of time for them (and that's not how you want to be remembered!). Try putting just one number. Which number? Use the number that is ALWAYS answered in a professional manner in a quiet, controlled setting. Do think twice about putting your cell phone number on there, unless you are very aware of where and how you answer it. At this point, every move you make is being evaluated. And your voicemail greeting should be professional as well. This is not the time to showcase your children's singing potential.

3. **Company name.** Look, you're not fooling anyone. No one believes you have a thriving consulting practice, so quit acting like it. "BUT," you'll say, "I'm open to consulting opportunities." Of course you are. And no one will not consider you just because you don't have a card that shows a company name with an LLC that you set up just in case a consulting opportunity came along. More often than not, consulting opportunities (when you're in the job search) come along as a result of meeting people, asking interesting questions and identifying a need.

4. **Printing on the back.** If you're like most people, you tend to write on the back of cards. So why did you just fill the entire backside up with half of your resume?

What you really want to do is put three areas of expertise on the **front** of the card. These may be functional areas or industries or a combination. A CFO who specializes in public companies may do something like: Sarbanes-Oxley, Treasury Management, Insurance. Or a VP of Marketing might have: Marketing Strategy, International, High Tech. A CEO may have: General Management, Turnarounds, Manufacturing. Give them a label to help them remember you. It doesn't necessarily have to be something you've done for years. If you're targeting a new industry, then put it on there! Who cares? It's just a card. If someone asks, you just say you're focused on that area.

5. **Flimsy paper and unclean edges.** Don't let something so small as perforated edges or lightweight paper (because, good for you, you just printed them off this morning on your crappy ink jet printer!) leave behind an impression that you're not quality. Use good card stock. I like to get cards from Vistaprint, because they have great designs (clean, professional ones – steer clear of the too-much ones), and the cards are printed on quality paper (80# cover stock is sufficient).

In short, your name, email (in lower case – because when you put capital letters in there, you're telling everyone that you don't understand the basic fundamentals of the Internet), phone and three areas of expertise. And that's it! Reduce the clutter. Increase the impact.

Your Email for the Job Search

1. **The address.** If you're using your personal email address for the job search, STOP! You'll have to admit, there are some really strange email addresses, and every time you send your resume or any email, your brand is

15

coming across. Does that brand accurately reflect your level of professionalism?

I recently saw such an email address, laxbill47@mail.com. If you didn't know that Bill was into Lacrosse, you might just think he's too lazy to work. And maybe he's 47 or was born in 1947. Another one I recently came across was snowleopard@mail.com. How can I take you seriously with that email? And then there's jedimaster@aol.com. Hey, is The Force hiring?

You never know the perception you're leaving with the person on the receiving end. Why risk it? The email you use should be firstlast@domain.com or first.last@domain.com. NEVER use the family email as your job search email.

And while I'm at it, let me mention a few other things that ruin your branding.

2. **The from line.** This shows me who the email is from before I ever look at it. The other day, I received an email from "Brian." This works if you're Cher or Madonna, but not if you're Brian. Do you have any idea how many Brians I know? I don't know if this is my good friend Brian, my distant friend Brian or the hundreds of other Brians I know in between. Depending on the subject line, I might just delete it without looking at the email – because it may just be from Spammer Brian. And I don't like him at all.

3. **Your signature line.** This gives me your contact information at the bottom of each email. The information here should be exactly what's on your business card. So often, people don't include their email in this area… and it drives me nuts. Because when I'm copying/pasting your contact info to the person you want to be introduced to, you make me go through an

extra step. Thanks a lot. You're now a drain on my time. No more intros for you!

4. **Your phone number.** While you're updating your resume and signature line with your new email, remember to list only one phone number (versus both home and cell). Which phone number should you list? Again, I don't really care which number you list. What I do care about is where and how you answer that phone.

If you're like most of us and answer your cell phone anywhere and everywhere (Like that woman did in the restroom the other day. I think the call could've waited.), then it's probably best to NOT put that number on your resume.

Use the phone that you will always answer in a quiet, professional setting. Don't forget the professional message, "Bill here, leave a message." is just like saying, "Hire me and I will wear cutoffs and flip flops every day." Which may be okay at some companies, but not before you get the job!

Don't let your lack of personal branding knock you out of the running. And if you think it won't, guess what. It probably already did.

A Great Handshake

There's a time and place to be memorable. This isn't one of them. Don't be known for a different handshake. Nobody appreciates it when you turn their wrist to put your hand on top. Nobody wants you to crunch their knuckles and remind them of the pain their older brother caused them all those years. Nobody likes the grandma handshake... not even your grandma! Use the same handshake for everyone you meet. That way, you'll either offend everyone or no one. Here's what a normal handshake consists of:

1. Extend arm

2. Use a firm (but not too tight) grip

3. Make eye contact

4. Double pump

5. Let go… please, please, please know when to let go

Nothing's worse than wearing out your welcome in the handshake. If you think you held on too long, the answer is yes, you did.

Being Prepared

Always bring something to take notes with. I am constantly amazed at the number of people who show up at a networking event, meeting or even an interview completely unprepared. I was having a conversation with Mike. An interesting person, he worked for a semiconductor company – in the automotive division. The company was figuring out how automotive manufacturers could incorporate its technology in music systems, sound decks and all things entertainment (because focusing on driving isn't entertainment enough?). Specifically, Mike was looking for companies with innovative technology to potentially acquire.

A couple of months before, I happened to meet someone who was working on some innovative technology in that same area. Perhaps it would benefit them to know each other? I told Mike about this company and the guy I met, and that they ought to connect. Mike told me he'd follow up with me. I asked Mike if he wanted to write the guy's name down (and maybe mine as well?). Obviously he didn't have a pen or a piece of paper. (Did he just show up at this event for the food?) He said, "That's okay, I'll remember it." No offense, Mike, but I have a strong feeling that after you polish down that second drink, meet about 15 other people, and catch up with some friends, you're not going to remember much. I'll do you a favor and write it down for you. I pulled out my stash of NetNotes (Networking Note Cards), wrote down the info, and handed it back to Mike. Now, he could choose to follow up… or not. His call.

Some of you may be wondering why Mike just didn't ask for my card? Sometimes I don't carry cards (maybe I'm secretly testing everyone to see if they're prepared with pen and paper!). I'm more interested in determining if I want your card than giving you mine. Others may be saying, "That would never happen to me, I have a great memory." So do I, but why chance it? If you write it down, you can free up your mind to remember something else (like the name of the person you just met!).

The next time you go to a networking event (by the way, every day in life is a networking event – even those things that don't appear at first glance to be a networking event – like grocery shopping, getting a pedicure/haircut, sitting on an airplane, standing in line… any line), be sure to be prepared. Always have paper and pen with you.

Never be left without the ability to write!

Molly's Takeaways

1. Get a professional-looking business card that shows your name, business phone number, email, and three areas of interest/expertise.
2. Make sure the signature line in your email has the same contact info as your business card.
3. Master the handshake.
4. Don't ever find yourself without a pen and paper.

Molly Wendell

CHAPTER 3: WHAT ARE YOU SUPPOSED TO DO IN LIFE?

How Tough Can a Job Search Really Be?

I had a conversation the other day with someone who was in the job search. Recruiters were giving her all kinds of bad advice – saying that her fifteen years of experience owning her own successful business was not useful to companies. She's trying to dumb down her skill set to match the job postings that are out there. And still, she's getting no response from this great job search tool called the Internet. Just last week, she heard back that she was overqualified for a position. And now, she doesn't know what to do.

Here's what you should do. Quit listening to people who have nothing good to say. Quit reading the news that sensationalizes how bad it is out there. Quit reading the job search jokes that are really not all that funny. Quit believing that you'll never find a job.

Sometimes this job search thing can be really tough. I mean **really** tough. Sometimes you break down. Sometimes you cry. When will it end? I really need a job. I mean, I have to find something, and I have to find it quick. I'm running out of money.

But what if you don't find something quick? What happens then? What happens when you go months longer than expected in a job search? What happens when you go years longer than expected in a job search? Then what?

I'll tell you what happens. You're still going to wake up each day, and you're going to get out of bed. And you're going to know that you once had it good, and you will again. And you're going to make today the best day ever because you've got a new attitude.

You've got nothing but opportunity ahead of you. And it's out there waiting for you... if only you would get a little bit creative.

I remember in the second year of my job search, I was volunteering on a political campaign. If my candidate won, I was going to Washington to work on his staff. I'd given my waking hours to that campaign with the hopes of creating a job for myself. I put all my eggs in one basket, and I was watching that basket closely!

About a week before the election, I was at an Executives Network job search meeting. When it came to my turn, I announced that if my candidate didn't win, I just didn't know what I was going to do. I mean, I had no other opportunities, no other options, no other ideas. Nothing. As I was sharing this grim outlook with everyone, my voice started to shake. Tears started forming in my eyes. I kept telling myself don't cry, don't cry, don't cry. I don't remember if I caught that single tear before it traveled down my cheek. But what I do remember was how quickly everyone in the room was there to offer support, ideas, advice, contacts, and hope.

I realized that day that I was probably not the only one having a tough time. I realized that others get tired, frustrated, lonely and depressed. But there was something greater in all of this. I realized then that it's the people who are going through the same situation – the job search – in a tough economy, who are going to stick with you for the rest of your life.

One week later, my candidate didn't win. I didn't go to Washington. And while I was coming to grips with the fact that I should have been putting all my eggs into many baskets... I worked with what I had. I came up with an idea based on someone I met during the campaign.

Within thirty days, I had four interviews for four completely different opportunities. And it put me on a path to a new career. As it turned out, the person I met on the campaign was instrumental in my landing the position I eventually got.

They say it's darkest just before dawn. Sometimes you have to get to a really low point in order to think creatively. When everything is going great, it's hard to be innovative. With limited resources, limited time, limited money, you're more likely to come up with the real breakthrough thinking.

Perhaps, though, you have some lessons you're supposed to learn in life. Perhaps you need to go through the struggles to better understand what others are going through. Or better appreciate what you had – and will have again. Perhaps, as a CFO, you can now appreciate the fact that getting rid of a big line item (as in people) doesn't necessarily make the business healthier, but it sure is easy to do. And maybe you'll think twice about how you "manage" the financials of the business. Perhaps you're in Human Resources, and you need to see how people who are in the job search sometimes get treated by HR… and you need to never be like that again!

If your job search is taking longer, if it's harder than you thought it would be, if the opportunities aren't coming to you like they used to – then it's time to get serious about your job search. It's time to get serious about yourself. It's time to take a long, hard look at who you are, and what you're doing. It's time to listen to others (who bring **positive** advice to the table). It's time to be open to new approaches. It's time to be open to new ideas of what your life might be. It's time to embrace the fact that you're in a position to figure out what you want to do with the rest of your life (or at least the next three to five years). Because the right thing is out there for you. You just may have some work to do before you're in a position to find the right position!

23

With your job being more than 50 percent of your life, I'm amazed how many people take a reactive approach to their job search. I guess it's not surprising, because most people I come in contact with tell me, "I've never had to look for a job in my life. Opportunities just came to me. This is the first time I've ever had to look for a job."

And I think, "Great, now maybe you'll take a strategic approach to your life."

What's the Perfect Position for You?

How much time have you spent really thinking about what you want to do in life? Forget about what you've always done. What do you really want to do?

How much time have you spent looking at you? What value do you bring a company? What are your skills? What experience have you had? What makes you uniquely positioned for a particular role?

One of the most interesting aspects of attending a job search meeting – where people go around the room and say who they are, what they're looking for, and how the group can help – is listening to the "who you are" aspect. I love listening to people's stories. Understanding what type of roles they've had. What kind of responsibilities they've held. What kind of accomplishments they realized. Couple that with what they want to do, and perhaps they're one step away from a new beginning!

Ever since I've known my friend, Steve, he's told me that he didn't particularly care for his job. He's good at it, but it doesn't pass the "get-out-of-bed" test every day. (He'd rather stay in bed than get up for that job.) Steve told me that he's thinking about leaving the company. I was thrilled for him.

I said, "That's great, what are you going to do?" He told me that some of his friends were starting a company selling to the same market – public sector. Immediately, I stopped him. "Steve, is that what you really want to do with your life? Sell products to the public sector? Is that really your idea of a good time?"

"Absolutely not!" he told me. But it was an opportunity to have an equity stake in a company. Again, Steve, not only are you headed right back to failing your get-out-of-bed test, you'll actually be more invested in it. Why waste your time? Why waste your friends' time?

I asked him what he really enjoyed. He said golf and international travel. In fact, he found a position working in sales for a golf course in Scotland – trying to get groups to book events there. We're getting closer, but we're still not there. The problem with that type of position is that although he'd get into the industry of choice, his travel would be limited.

Steve, what if you were to start your own company where you go to five or ten courses and be a "manufacturer's rep" of sorts? Market the events to groups of people – and plan golf trips for them. Plus, you could start a monthly newsletter called "Best Golf Vacations." Research the courses and tell the good, the bad and the ugly about each one. Help people make a decision as to where they need to go.

There you go. You could travel. You could play golf. You could have 100 percent equity in your company. And more than likely, you wouldn't even need to worry about the get out of bed test, because you probably wouldn't ever go to sleep!

How about that for your life? Wouldn't that be fun?

And Steve said, "Yes, that would be perfect." Well great! Go do it! And until you do, I don't want to hear another word about how much you hate your job!

Here's the question for you. What is your passion? What have you always wanted to do? Maybe you've always wanted to own your own business. Maybe you really love working for others. Either way, take a look at what you enjoy, and position yourself right in the middle of it.

Give your life the time it deserves to think about this. Don't rush into another company. Sometimes it's a travesty when people land too quickly, because they neglect to go through this process.

Who Are You Supposed to Be?

They say it's one of the hardest things to figure out. And many people go through their entire lives without ever figuring it out. But, I don't think it's that hard. I think deep down, you actually know. Deep down, you know exactly what you've always wanted to do. Maybe you're scared to admit it. Maybe even a little bit embarrassed to admit it. I can't tell you how many times I've been talking to someone about their job search – and finally, finally after thirty minutes, they'll say, "You know what I really want to do? I want to start my own pet accessories business." And I think, great! What are you waiting for? Start it! "But I don't have the capital. I don't have the resources." Well, I don't have the time to hear all of your excuses, because I'm already thinking that this is a great idea. It's a great idea because it's something you want to do. So go do it. You don't have to have everything in place. You don't need perfection. You just need the green light. Well, here it is. Go for it! What do you have to lose?

I really believe that deep down, we all have something we've always wanted to do. And when you're in the job search – now is the time. Perhaps you were put in a job search to be given this time to put this plan in place. Don't waste it by scattering your energies looking for another job. Go make your life happen right now! And, if it doesn't work out, at least you can say you tried it.

A friend of mine who, by the way, is FINALLY on track to doing what she's supposed to do in life, was telling me about her on-again-off-again training for this new field of hers.

I finally asked her, "What is your problem? It's so obvious that you're supposed to do this. What's holding you back? What are you scared of?"

And she said, "I'm scared of the success that I'll have." Which I think is a complete cop out of an answer. You're scared of what?! That has to be one of the dumbest things I've ever heard (sorry!). I've heard of being scared of failure. Many people are scared of failure. But scared of success? Well, why don't you go be successful and see how frightened you become? I'm taking bets that it won't scare you at all.

Now, let's look at failure. Ask Einstein, Lincoln, Dyson (yes, the vacuum cleaner guy – love those vacuums) about failure. So what if you fail? What's the worst thing that could happen? Are you alive? Are you healthy? Are you completely stressed out? Yes. Yes. Yes. But did you learn something in the process? Perhaps your failing enterprise opened up a new window of opportunity. One that you wouldn't have had knowledge of had you not tried this new venture. So, go ahead. Fail a little bit. Don't be afraid.

I've met a few people who've had their own businesses but decided for one reason or another to embark on a job search. It's usually because their business isn't going so well, or they need more capital to make it to the next milestone. This reminds me of Manuel. Manuel showed up at one of the Executives Network job search meetings and told everyone about his business – which sounded amazing to all of us. The niche he created, the opportunity, it's actually quite innovative and exciting.

Then, in the next breath, he told us that he's looking for a new position in Supply Chain Management, because the business wasn't doing so great. I asked Manuel, "If the business was doing well, would you still be looking to get a new job?"

And he said, "No." Which immediately told me (and anybody else within earshot) he's looking for all of the wrong reasons.

So I didn't want to help him find a new job. I wanted to help him find some talent, resources and motivation to stick with what he had and make it successful. Turns out, all Manuel needed was a little bit of motivation, and some help from others in the group. And in just a few months, Manuel took the business to a whole new level. And he's actually happy. He's excited for the opportunity. But he almost gave up… again, for all of the wrong reasons.

I'm sure you've heard it plenty of times, "Don't throw the baby out with the bath water." If you have an interesting business and you really enjoy it, but you're dealing with financial struggles, don't quit on it. Maybe you just need some other minds to help you through it. Find others with different functional areas of expertise, and ask them to give you some pro-bono consulting advice. People in the job search love to do this because it keeps their skills sharp. Besides, it's always good to feel needed. Don't deny them that opportunity to help you out. Don't deny you that opportunity to let them help you out.

Sometimes the path you go down... isn't always the one you're supposed to stay on. In my third year of commercial real estate, I started going to a business coach. I walked in there and proudly said, "Look, I'm really happy doing what I'm doing. I have no desire to quit my job or do any crazy life changes. All I need help with is improving performance. My activity level is sky high, but my performance is average. In order to double performance, do I need to double my activity? If that's the answer, I can't. I'm just exhausted."

During our third session, he said something to me that was life changing. He made a comment about control – and how it was one of his greatest strengths. All of a sudden, it hit me like a ton of bricks. "Oh no," I said, "I have to quit my job!" I guess I caught him by surprise. I guess I caught myself by surprise.

At that moment, I realized that the ability to control things was one of my greatest strengths. In my current job, I basically controlled nothing. The building owner and company controlled what really happened on the deal. At any point in time, the building owner could lease the space to someone else. At any point in time, the company could decide that they weren't moving. I was in the middle – basically a translator. And while a commercial real estate broker provides far more value than that, they are not the decision maker. I didn't really ever have control of a deal.

This concept was causing me so much hidden stress. I had no idea. I get so much satisfaction out of controlling things, and here I am controlling nothing. Therefore, no job satisfaction. What a realization! I immediately started looking for other opportunities.

About six months after I left commercial real estate, still trying to figure out what I was going to do with my life, I went to Jerusalem to work on an archeology dig. I'd never done that and thought it might be kind of interesting. Plus, I'd meet people from all over the world. One day on the dig, I had my pickax aimed at a fresh piece of ground… heaving away. And I was thinking, what do I really enjoy? If I had to pick one thing, what would it be?

Networking. I love networking. I love meeting new people. I love connecting people. I love teaching people how to network. I love everything about it. It was right then I knew that I would build a business around the concept of networking. And since it was my own business… I'd have all the control in the world. Lucky me!

The path of commercial real estate made me realize what was important to me. And it enabled me to veer off it completely to get where I needed to be.

How Do You Find the Right Job for You?

But what if you don't want to start your own company? It's not for everyone. It consumes your life. It's risky. It's stressful. What if you really enjoy working for others and want to continue to do so? How do you find the right job for you? How do you compete effectively in today's marketplace?

So many books have been written about this. Plenty of places offer career assessments. I remember when I was at IBM Corporation, we had an online application called Careers. It was really interesting. You were given 90 scenarios. And you gave it a "most like me," "least like me," or somewhere in between. After answering all, it came up with the career you're most suited for. I was pretty excited when it said I should be a publisher of a magazine. I love magazines. I love being the boss. Maybe it would've been better to take the quiz before going to work for IBM?

I haven't been able to find this application, but there are plenty of others out there. One I like in particular was in the *National Business Employment Weekly* in the early '90s. It's a Brain Dominance test that figures out which side of the brain you prefer to work with, and gives you career ideas based on that. If you're interested, a more up-to-date brain dominance tool, mentioned previously, is Emergenetics.

A lot of people read *What Color is Your Parachute?* But, to be honest with you, I've found that simply talking to lots of people –

and asking them about what they do — is one of the best ways to gain some insight. Think about the industries you might go into. Talk to people who are in that business. Ask everyone you know, "Do you love what you do?" Then ask why. See if they come up with some of the same answers you might. You might find some fascinating industries and positions. And... you might find some you want to steer clear of in a big way!

Molly's Takeaways

1. Identify your passion and how you can position yourself to profit from it.
2. Don't be afraid to fail. Edison conducted thousands of experiments before he got the light bulb right.
3. Perceived dead ends can often lead to the right doors opening.
4. Reassess your aptitudes to identify your strengths and decide what you really want to do.

Molly Wendell

CHAPTER 4: TARGETING YOUR MARKET

Are You Managing Your Job Search to Produce the Greatest Returns?

I was visiting my friend, Mike, in New York recently. Mike is a trader on the commodities exchange. He's been trading for more than twenty years, and success at trading comes naturally for him. Well, perhaps on the surface. It wasn't always that way. We got to talking about his early days as a trader. He remembers a time when he was pretty lousy at it. He came very close to quitting. Then one day, he was watching some other, more senior traders. He started to see a pattern. They were heads down – managing each individual trade. Rarely did they come up for air to analyze their overall portfolio.

It was at that moment Mike realized what he needed to do to be successful in the business. In that instant, perfect clarity. He knew what he'd been doing wrong. He was so caught up in analyzing his overall portfolio that he was neglecting the individual trades. Quit worrying about the big picture, and start drilling in on each individual trade. Make each individual trade profitable, and the entire portfolio will have a greater return on investment. Sounds pretty obvious right? But, it got me thinking about how most people proceed through life.

When you have a big project, break it down, they say (whoever 'they' are). When you're learning to read and you have a three-syllable word in front of you, just sound it out, your teacher says (or in my case, my sister, Betsy). This got me thinking about job search. We get so focused on the big picture – the monumental task of landing the perfect job – we forget to drill down on the individual activities that will produce a greater return on investment (i.e., great job offers).

If you're currently in the search (or about to be but don't know it yet), you might want to think about how you're approaching your search. Are you so focused on just getting a job that you're neglecting to manage the activities that will lead to it? What are these activities? You may be thinking, "Well, I have to get my resume in order. I have to get online and look at who's hiring. I have to tell everyone I know that I'm looking. I have to contact recruiters. Now I have to redo my resume because one person made a comment about it." No you don't! You don't have to do any of this. If you're focused on these activities, you're going to produce the worst returns ever recorded in history!

Why don't you start with the end in mind? How do you get a job offer? No matter how much time you spend sitting in front of the computer, chances are really good that without face-to-face interaction, an offer won't be showing up in your inbox anytime soon. You'll probably have to actually meet someone at a company and build a relationship. So how do you meet people at companies? You'll probably have to get out of your house and network. Where will you network? Depends on what type of role you're looking for.

It's safe to say that if you're meeting lots of people, building great relationships, and through smart questioning identifying needs/problems and determining your ability to solve them – your chances of being considered for opportunities should be great. If you're not uncovering needs, you're not asking enough questions. If you're uncovering lots of needs and not figuring out how you can solve them, you're either hanging out with the wrong people or your capabilities might be less than desirable.

Quit focusing on the activities that don't matter, and start focusing on the ones that do – interacting with people. Manage these interactions carefully. Learn from each individual interaction and make improvements with the next one. Through this process, you'll be carrying on intelligent conversations about interesting problems that would be fascinating to solve. It won't take long before the offers start coming. And once you've perfected this technique, the offers never actually stop. And when you step back and take a look at the big picture, your overall portfolio of opportunities will have incredible returns. How's that for your very own bull market?

Why Do We Spend More Time Preparing for a Water Landing Than a Job Search?

Every time I get on an airplane (which is quite frequently these days), the flight attendants go through the same emergency drill. Not once have I had to open the emergency exit door, but I've had more instructions on what to do in the event of a water landing than most people have had in practicing their own job search drill. And guess which one happens more frequently?

Embarking on a job search is not something you do every day. It's not something you expect to do frequently. And it's certainly not something you think to (or want to?) become an expert in. But chances are really good that in today's environment, you can expect to embark on multiple job searches over the course of your career, regardless of age.

This is probably not big news. How is it, then, that so many people have no clue how to go about looking for a job? It's as though they thought they were immune. They thought people would just call them up and offer them new positions. Maybe it was like that in the past, but it's just not that way anymore.

This is mostly what I hear from people:

- "I haven't been in a job search in – forever."

- "I can't remember the last time I had to actually look for a job."
- "I've never had to actually look for a job."

35

- "Every job I ever got just came to me without trying."

When I question these people about what they want to do, it seems like they're "just in the early stages – so they're not quite focused yet." Is that how they prepared for a big meeting when they were working? If so, no wonder they're looking for work!

And, if you're not currently in the search, you will be at one point in your life. Why don't you take a little time and start mapping out a plan for your job search? Here are some basic things to think about:

1. **Position/job desired.** What do you want to do? I mean what do you really want to do? Not what have you done for the last thirty years. What do you want to do for next five to ten (or even one to three) years? Help us help you by giving us some focus on what you want to do.

2. **Industry.** Which industries do you want to work in? What are the attributes of these industries – and what are some other industries that share these characteristics? Maybe that will lead you to some new ideas. And don't say that your skills are transferable, so industry doesn't really matter. That's just a cop out for not doing your homework.

3. **Company size.** Are you a large company person, a startup player or maybe focused on medium sized companies? And if so, what is a medium sized company to you? Is it $100 Million or anything less than $1 Billion? You need to think hard about the type of organization in which you excel. Think about the environment in which you enjoy working. Is it global, national or local? Centralized or decentralized? Do you

prefer working in the corporate office or at the branch office? Set some parameters to help weed out some companies and bring others to the surface.

4. **Location.** There's a direct correlation between length of time in the job search and geographic target. The longer you're in the search, the more the geographic scope increases. It is not uncommon to have a corporate role that's not housed at the corporate office (this is especially true for those roles where you'll travel a lot). Be open to opportunities in other cities. You never know who you might meet on the plane on the way over and back. I remember interviewing in Philadelphia for a position. In the interview, I was told that the company had two positions that might be interesting for me. One in Philly and the other in Scottsdale, Arizona – three traffic lights from my house. Had I not been open to relocating, I would've never known about the opportunity right in my own backyard. Then, on the plane ride home, I ended up getting a lead from the guy sitting next to m. And that's ultimately how I found my next job.

5. **Target companies.** Maybe you're telling people that you're open to any company –you just want to work in a growing industry, for a company that treats its employees above and beyond. Well, it's really hard to help you here. As my sixth grade teacher used to tell me, "To be specific is terrific. To be vague is the plague." Think about who you would like to work for. What do those companies look like, but more importantly, what are the names of those companies? Again, don't be lazy and unprepared. Don't make your network figure out where you want to work.

Now, you might be saying, "But really I am open to opportunities and I don't want to limit myself." The only way you're going to limit yourself is by not being prepared. Because the more targeted and prepared you are to give others a frame of reference in which to think, the more they can come up with additional ideas for you.

Quit acting like your job search is going to sneak up on you. Start preparing for it right now. Go through your own job search drill. And practice. Practice. Practice. It will get you that much closer to a successful landing.

Targeting an Industry: Does Your Target Industry Mean What You Think it Means?

In one of our Executives Network meetings, Adam was describing his target industry. He said he'd like to work in the service industry. That's perfect if everyone knows what the "service industry" means. When you say service industry to me, my mind immediately thinks of dry cleaners. When I proudly announced that it was a great idea, and that industry could possibly use someone with his skills, he was less than overjoyed. I didn't get it. Didn't he say that's what he was targeting? Apparently, in his mind, the service industry is quite different – and doesn't necessarily include Dry Cleaners USA.

This same thing happened in another meeting. Someone was targeting "broadband." But apparently, this broadband world is much more granular than I'm aware (which is fine), but it doesn't help me help him if he doesn't get specific about where the differences lie.

Every time someone mentions insurance, I cringe. I know there are companies that do commercial, personal, auto, property and casualty, life, health, and probably a ton of others, but how am I supposed to know which one does which? I'm not in that world!

The only time I have a clue is when the company ends in the word "life" (thanks MetLife... I know what you do!).

It happened again when someone mentioned she was targeting entertainment. Did you mean the movies, television, cinemas, amusement parks, concerts, sports franchises, or perhaps that coupon book that everyone tries to sell to me at the beginning of each year?

This got me thinking... how many of you target an industry that you believe is very specific and focused, and the rest of us come up with all kinds of ideas that are completely beyond the scope of what you're looking for?

I've said it before (and no doubt, I'll say it again!), as my sixth grade teacher taught me, "To be specific is terrific. To be vague is the plague."

When you're targeting an industry, be sure to get very specific... right down to the company size. Mentioning a few companies in that space would be helpful too. Maybe something like this:

"I'm targeting companies in the entertainment space, specifically cinema chains. Targets include AMC, Regal Cinemas, Landmark, ArcLight, and IMAX. Additionally, I'd entertain companies that sell technology to them – or are in the consumer entertainment/screen space. Companies like Sony, Panasonic, Samsung, Saaria, MicroCRT, Cinedigm and 3ality."

This is something I can work with. It's quite possible that I might know someone from at least one of these companies, or maybe even a couple. If not, perhaps I could recommend a contact of someone who works with one of them, maybe a distributor, a supplier, a charity, a customer, or even someone who used to work there.

If you find that you're giving target industries and aren't getting many contacts from others, your search may be too general. Get specific for us so we can help you. After all, you might not want to work for Dry Cleaners USA!

Another Overused Job Search Phrase: "I'm Willing to Relocate"

Maybe you're one of them. One of those people who say, "I'm in the job search and I'm willing to relocate." And maybe you're one of those same people who continue to network in the city you're already in. No offense, but your strategy sucks! The job you're looking for in Philadelphia is not here in Los Angeles. It's in Philadelphia. Are you looking to network with German companies in the solar industry? Then go to Germany and meet them!

Sometimes the old "I'm willing to relocate" line doesn't come out until you've been in the search for a while. You see, the longer you're in the search, the larger the geographic target a search seems to encompass. Often, I see people newly out of work who come into a job search meeting and say, "I want to work within a ten-mile radius of my house in Chicago." In some cities you can actually do that. In others, not so much. But here's the thing. After about a month of not finding anything within that ten-mile radius (and not looking all that hard in my opinion), the geographic scope begins to widen. "I want to work within a 30-minute commute – which could be anything downtown or near the airport." Another month goes by, and then, "I've decided to open up the scope to the greater Chicago area, including the north and west suburbs." Another month. "Anywhere in the Midwest – within a one-hour plane flight from O'Hare." Another month goes by. "I'm open to anything east of the Mississippi." Pretty soon, you're down to, "English-speaking countries or a place where I can find a translator."

If you're really interested and open to relocation, quit saying those magical words… I'm willing to relocate. And start doing something that actually is magic. Disappear. I mean disappear to the cities in which you're interested in relocating.

When I think about my own job search years ago, I was willing to relocate. Where I really erred was that I was too open on "where." The reality is that people are out of work in every city. Why would I think I'm well-positioned or even somewhat positioned to get an interview, let alone land a job, halfway across the country when I don't even know what's going on halfway across the country? I was lucky I got the first meeting.

I had an opportunity in Chicago. It was through a recruiter. I knew the company. If I was smart, I would've made my way out there, started networking, and meeting with all kinds of people in the industry. Then, if that job hadn't come through (which it didn't, by the way), I might have networked my way into some other opportunities. But instead, I tried to phone in my presence. And that's just not very smart. No wonder they didn't hire me!

In the book *Team of Rivals*, about Abraham Lincoln, there's a great story about the importance of getting out there and meeting people. Lincoln was relatively unknown and ended up winning the Republican nomination (hopefully that's not new news to you!). One of his competitors, Samuel Chase, didn't want to travel. Instead, he spent most of his campaign in the comfort of his own living room.

Instead of visiting his potential constituents, he decided to write letters to as many people as he could (today's equivalent to shooting off a bunch of emails instead of having actual in-person conversations). Whereas Lincoln spent all of his time traveling around. Meeting people. Basically networking! When it came time to "hire" the candidate, guess which one got selected. So, who are you more like? Chase or Lincoln?

41

If I were to do it over again, I'd learn from all of this. I'd do "willing to relocate" very differently. Here's what I recommend to those who are really willing to relocate:

1. Target two to three cities where you really want to live.

2. Subscribe to the local *Business Journal* and read every issue cover to cover.

3. Identify networking events in those cities. Pick a week where there are three to four events that you're interested in attending. Be sure to include job search networking events.

4. Find people in your network who know people in those cities. Get one-on-one networking meetings with them. I'd bet those people know people. They all have coworkers (current and former), neighbors, friends and acquaintances. Tap into their networks.

5. Book a flight… and stay with a friend (save some money).

6. Fly out to your target city, attend the networking and job search events – and hope to find a couple more while you're there. Also, figure out what events are coming up that will require an additional trip. Do your one-on-one meetings, and try to get a few more while you're there.

7. Hang out at Starbucks while you're in between meetings. See if you might meet some other people. Maybe even take a class. Get there early. You'll meet some locals and make new friends (who probably know people as well!). See if any of the hotels have a national

conference in town... hang out at their lobby bar during the evenings to meet people from the conference.

8. Repeat this process each month until you end up there.

Are you really serious about being open to relocation? Then you need to get really serious about relocating. Quit talking about it and start doing something. Get out there. Find out what's happening. Quit using mental telepathy (or email) and start having actual, in-person conversations with people in those cities. You'll know you're doing it right when no one realizes you're from out of town. And if you do end up moving there, you'll already have some friends. How's that for a bonus?

"I Wouldn't Mind Working There" and Other Phrases to Never Use in the Job Search

I was interviewed by a news station in Denver. The reporter asked me if it was okay, when targeting a company or position, to say, "I'd like to do this type of job, but if that's not available, I'd be willing to do this." My answer... emphatically no!

Phrases like this drive me insane:

- "I'd be willing to work there."

- "I wouldn't be opposed to it."

- "It would be okay."

- "It wouldn't be my first choice, but it would be fine."

- "I guess I could do that job."

It may come as a surprise to you, but no company wants to hear, "I'd be willing to work for you."

43

I would never hire someone that "wouldn't mind" working for me. By all means, don't let me inconvenience you by hiring you! I also don't want anyone who will work anywhere. If you're so desperate, it means you yourself haven't qualified the companies. And your mediocre interest just might translate into mediocre performance. Thanks, but no thanks.

But wait, you say. You would **never** tell a company such things. You would **never** actually say to a company, "I wouldn't mind working for you". Of course you wouldn't say those words to them (yet, you would to your network!). But if you're thinking it, it's coming out in some other form… be it your body language, your level of enthusiasm and interest, your communications. It's there. You're not that good an actor!

Quit being a mediocre planner of your job search. Figure out where exactly you want to work. Bring some passion to the search. Target those companies with careful thought. Be one of those people who use phrases such as:

- "I absolutely want to work here!"

- "This is the place for me!"

- "I've done all of the research and this is where I add the most value."

- "I'm your next shining star!"

My friend Tom told me about a recent interview. He was meeting with a Senior Vice President regarding a first-line managerial position. While this position was a few levels below his target position, he was very excited about the company. When the hiring manager asked him why he was even interested in this low-level position, Tom told him he had researched where the puck was headed in technology, mapped it to his strengths, and said, "I'm targeting three segments… and your company is at the intersection of these segments. It's where I want to work. I want to get on the bus… and we can figure out down the road where I sit."

The hiring manager liked what he heard and is now considering Tom for a role that wasn't even posted – and probably never would have been. This new role is higher level and more appropriately matched with Tom's skills. This is what happens when you're meeting with the right people – those who have the power to make decisions that are good for the company.

Tom took the focus away from the concept of, "I'd be willing to take this position to get into the company" and turned it into, "This is where I want to be. We can figure out the details later."

Here's what Tom did that's different from what most others do. Tom knew where he needed to be. He did the research. He figured out where the opportunity would be. He looked at his own strengths – and came up with the best fit. This is before he'd ever gotten in the door.

When it comes to job search, how many people really do their homework? How many people have a well-thought-out plan before asking others for help? I can tell you right now, the answer is not enough of you! Because if you did, you would have more success in your networking meetings. You would have more success in your interviews. And you would have more success in your job search.

Take the time to really figure out what you want to do. Find out who you want to be. Put together a thoughtful target list of who you want to work for (not just the companies that have an opening). And create some positive energy around it by saying, "This is who I am. This is my dream job. These are the companies I absolutely want to work for." You'll be amazed how much this newfound positive energy will do to get you on the right track to find the right fit. And you may even find more than one company that "wouldn't mind" having you on board!

My Skills Are Transferable... Right?

So many people in the job search say, "I don't want to focus on any one industry because I believe my skills are transferable." Guess what? No one else does. What if someone told you your skills weren't transferable? What would you do then? Why do you think so many companies tell recruiters, "I want a CIO from our industry who worked for one of the following companies." That's all they're doing. Pulling people from the competition!

And here you are trying to sell them on why you're a better fit – without any industry experience. Well, guess what. They're not buying! And they're not going to risk losing the search because "they weren't listening and kept bringing in candidates who didn't meet the spec." But there is an exception to this rule. There is one time in your life when your skills are transferable.

Midway through my two-year search, I met a woman who just landed a VP of Marketing role for a technology company. Wow, I thought. That's the job I'm looking for! She must have a really great background in running marketing for technology companies! When I asked her how long she'd been in the technology industry, she told me she hadn't. I had eighteen years in the industry. When I asked her where she was a VP of Marketing previously, she said she wasn't. She came from the agency side. I had been a VP of Marketing at three previous companies. When I asked her how she found the position, she told me she knew the president. And at that moment, my life changed. It was eye-opening. After getting over the fact that she pretty much stole my job, I started to think about what she did that I didn't. She networked her way into the job. And from then on, that's exactly what I decided to do.

If you're going to network your way into a job that you're not qualified for (at least on paper), then you really have to figure out what it will take to make them want you. I found that if I asked enough smart questions, people thought I knew their industry. Soon, it led to offers where I was stealing someone else's job. So quit trying to sell others on why your skills are transferable. Show them that it has nothing to do with your background, and everything to do with how you think and approach problems. Start asking smart questions. You'll be amazed into which new industries it will lead you.

How Do I Transition Into a New Industry? Maybe It's Just Pure Luck.

As I've traveled throughout the country, attending our Executives Network job search meetings, I realized that the same conversations were taking place regardless of city. What they talked about in Chicago – they talked about in Silicon Valley. The thoughts on people's minds in Dallas were the same thoughts in Phoenix. And that's when I got the idea that we had to get everyone in the same "virtual" room and take the conversation further.

Executives Network had its first national teleconference. Lots of people around the country talking about a specific topic - in this case, alternative energy. We wanted to answer questions like: How do I transition into this industry? Who are the players? What are the opportunities? What can I learn from others targeting the same industry as me?

Michael, an EN Member, was our featured guest. He talked about how he successfully transitioned into the solar industry. What he DIDN'T do was sit at the computer and search for job postings all day. What he DID do – took a little more effort, but was far more effective.

Michael networked his way to the job! (I know, networking, big surprise! You don't think I'd feature anyone who got a job from a job posting? Has anyone ever gotten a higher-level job from a posting ?)

When he first decided to target solar, he read up on the industry. Then, he did the smartest thing a job seeker could do. He turned the computer off! He got out and attended every solar and alternative energy event he could find. He went to local get-togethers, regional meetings, national conferences.

A couple of months into his search, he started sporting the nametag "Solar Mike" at every event. His reputation soon grew – as someone obviously in the solar industry. Why else would he wear a nametag like that? If people asked, he would just tell them he was really passionate about solar. After all, it's only a nametag.

All told, he met with more than 200 people in the industry. And it was through one of those meetings, with one of his target companies that he landed the perfect job in solar. Do you think he was lucky? Maybe. But as my college friend, Maurice, always used to say, "Luck comes to those who work hard to make it happen."

Michael certainly worked hard to make his luck happen.

He had much to share with the group about the process of transitioning into solar. But three things he said struck me as great lessons for anyone – regardless of the industry you're pursuing:

1. **Some will. Some won't. So what.** Some people will be very helpful. In fact you'll be surprised how much people will help you. On the other hand, some won't be helpful at all. So what? Move on.

2. **Never underestimate the power of someone else's network.** Every time you're given a lead, pursue those

opportunities. You have no idea who these people know – or who their network knows. Pursue all leads diligently. The lead you never followed up on could have been the one that led you to your dream job. Can you afford to chance it?

3. **"I'm one networking contact away from finding my dream job."** Continue to motivate and reinforce your networking effort by reminding yourself of just that! Remember, you don't need to find ten positions, you just need to find one. The right one.

If you're planning to transition to another industry, then do yourself a favor, and get relevant. Get embedded in that industry. Get to know the companies. Get to know the players. Arm yourself with knowledge and contacts so that, despite the fact that you have no industry experience, you know what's going on.

Just remember, the more people you talk to, the more information you'll find, the more companies you'll discover, the more opportunities you'll uncover. Put in some serious effort – and increase your odds of being truly lucky!

What Makes You Different...
I Mean Really Different?

If I sit in one more job search networking meeting and listen to some CIO tell me what makes him different is that, "I work with people, process and technology...", I think I'll scream. Here's what I'll scream, "Who doesn't? In this day and age, who doesn't work with people, process and technology? That doesn't make you different! It makes you exactly like every other person in the room. It doesn't matter what functional area you're from. Virtually everyone works with people, process and technology."

The same goes for the VP of Sales. "I build and mentor sales team to reach their highest potential."

"And that makes you different? Isn't that the entry point for every person in sales management?" Give us a little help here. Are you best at working with highly technical sales teams with long sales cycles and average orders in the multi-millions? Maybe you excel with managing channel partners in consumer products – where you're trying to penetrate big-box stores? Give us those details... and maybe we can help.

What about the VP of Human Resources? "I'm an HR generalist, working with all aspects of HR." Guess what? Most of us non-HR types don't really know what that means. Tell us specifically, are you best when companies are in the early stages – ramping up from 30 people to 300? Do you work well with part-time and/or unionized labor? Maybe your specialty is full-time, technical workforces. Do you know how to decrease attrition to all-time record lows in a call-center environment? If so, we may have some ideas for you.

Oh, VP of Marketing, don't think you're going to get off easy. "I build brands." What are you, Coca-Cola? Companies that are hurting in revenue aren't worried about building their brand (and creating the best company newsletter ever), they're worried about driving sales. How are you going to affect that? Let us know. We'd love to hear it.

Finance, Ops, R&D, Engineering, General Management. The same goes for all of you. Tell us how you're repositioning and repackaging yourself in today's competitive marketplace. Tell us what makes you different... really different.

As I listen to people's backgrounds, I attempt to reposition people by looking for what I call combinable skills. What skills can you combine that make you very valuable? My brother-in-law worked as a chef in a fine-dining restaurant. He's now a sales rep for a food distributor (and you guessed it... he too works with people, process and technology!). He sells food to chefs. They respect him because they know he was a great chef, and he understands their issues. He doesn't focus on what food they want to purchase. He talks to them about the menu (thereby determining the ingredients required). He makes recommendations as to things that will work well together. He gets it. They like that he gets it. They buy from him. He likes that they buy from him.

Think about your background. What in your background can you combine that enables you to reposition and differentiate yourself? Maybe you run marketing and have worked with both consumer and business-to-business products. Try looking for a company that sells in the B2B world... but is trying to penetrate the B2C space.

Maybe you're in Operations and you've worked in semiconductor manufacturing, plus spent some years in the lighting industry. Combine that with your stint in construction when you were working part-time in college, and you just might be the perfect Ops exec in the solar industry.

Were you a CIO for a retailer that had multi-unit locations? Why not take that multi-location concept and check out opportunities in the consumer banking industry (it may be tough times right now... but great companies are always looking for great talent). Did you run sales for a radio station that focuses on the Hispanic market? Find a consumer-based company that is targeting the Hispanic market where mass media is a critical component and make your pitch.

Can't figure out which industries might be good fits for your combined skills? Try playing this game with others from different backgrounds. I call it "Guess the Industry." Describe the attributes of the industries you've worked in and see what that means to other people. You'll be amazed at the answers they come up with. And it might lead you to some new and exciting companies to target… companies where you can take your combined set of skills, and reposition yourself as someone who really is different!

Think about your background and try to steer toward a position that will make you the only person uniquely qualified for the job. Let's say you have international experience. And you've been in retail industry. Plus you've spent some time selling technology. And finally, you worked for company that creates shopping carts for online resellers. Take all of these components, combine them, and maybe you can find:

- The international firm that sells technology to retail. It could be point-of-sale systems, scanners, customer data, websites, software.

- The retailer that sells technology products internationally but wants to expand into the online world.

- The retailer that sells technology products in one geographic market that wants to expand internationally.

- The technology company that sells to retailers – and wants to open up internationally.

- The technology company selling to retailers – that doesn't have an online offering – but perhaps should.

Don't worry that the company doesn't have a job posting. They don't know you're out there. They don't know the perfect person is ready, willing and able to take on that challenge for them. Do them a favor and make yourself visible.

How Do I Find These Companies That Are Doing All of These Things?

The best way to find out is to talk to people. When you read it in the paper, it's old news. Everyone else already knows. You want to find out about the things that no one knows about. The only way to do that is to talk to people. But why would they tell me, you ask? That's easy. Because you're going to ask. You're going to ask in a way that will not only get you the information, but position you as the expert!

Don't think that you're going to hit the jackpot with the first person that you meet. You don't have enough data to be competitive yet. You need to ask many people. Many, many people. I mean a lot of people! How many people? At least 25. Maybe 50. It might take 200. But you're going to get conversations with each and every one of them. You're going to learn what's going on. You're going to find out about the trends in the industry. You're going to get up to speed on the challenges the industry faces. You'll take a look at the players and find out who's doing what. You'll find out who are the suppliers, the buyers, the substitutes. You're going to figure out who's effective in what submarket. Who's positioned for the coming years.

You're going to know it all. And with all of that information, you're going to be able to make an informed decision about which segment you want to be in. Who you want to work for. And what you want to do.

You might find that the most interesting companies are not the leaders in their industry. Remember Avis? "We're #2. We try harder." At that point, Avis was probably a more interesting company to work for than Hertz because it was trying to innovate itself to grab the top spot. And look at the business now. National is going after the green/alternative segment. Budget lets you walk into a rental car lot and pick out your own car and drive away. Who would have ever thought you could do that? Enterprise will pick you up. Nice!

When I was looking to get into commercial real estate, I didn't really know what the industry looked like. The bad news was that there was no "book" of the industry. The good news is that it seemed like everyone I ran across knew someone in the industry. I started scheduling meetings with anyone and everyone. I didn't care where they worked or what they did, if they were in the commercial real estate industry, I wanted to meet with them.

I would ask the following questions, starting typically with the phrase, "Tell me a little bit about..."

1. What you do?

2. What types of people and companies do you interact with?

3. What types of firms are in this industry? What does each one do?

4. Where does your firm fit in the overall picture?

5. Who are your biggest competitors? It was always funny to me – when I'd hear, "Oh, my biggest competition is Brickstone Commercial." Then, when I met someone from Brickstone, they didn't even mention the other company as a dot on their competitive radar. It happened all the time! And it really helped me get a feel for who the real players were!

6. Who's doing interesting things?

7. Who's expanding? Who's contracting? Why?

8. Who are your largest customers?

9. What about partnerships?

10. Who are the people in the industry that are driving change? Oh, do you know that person? Oh, I'd love to meet with them. Can you help me with that? Great!

11. Who are the people to stay away from?

12. Who are others I should meet with that will give me some great insight?

13. What are the opportunities in this industry?

14. What are the challenges? Is it profit? Revenue? Capital? Operations?

15. What does it take to do your job effectively?

Through this questioning, I was able to map out the industry, identify the strong players, and handpick the role I wanted, at the company I wanted to work for. It can be an incredible high when you know you're doing what you're supposed to do in life! Sometimes you get down a path and realize it's the wrong one. But that's okay… as long as you learn from it!

Molly's Takeaways

1. Prepare for your search by targeting your industry, company, and dream position – be specific.
2. Network and ask questions until you know enough to sound like an expert.
3. If you're willing to relocate, start with where you want to be.
4. Be like Solar Mike, and make your luck happen.

Molly Wendell

CHAPTER 5: THE RESUME

Nobody Cares About Your Resume

Quit sending your resume to everyone you know in hopes that they "know of a job that's perfect for you." A friend asked me to review her resume. With a deep sigh, I said sure. What I really wanted to say was that nobody cares about your resume. Your resume is never going to get you a job. Quit wasting your time hanging out with that piece of work-in-process paper and start hanging out with real live people who may know people that will help you land your next opportunity.

A perfect resume simply doesn't exist. But is it good enough? Do you feel good about it? Then, great. Move on.

Too often, job seekers hide behind the resume thinking it's the perfect calling card to get in the door. They lead with their resume all of the time. They send emails with their resume attached. They make phone calls saying, "I'll send you my resume." Even others get on board with the concept when the job seeker calls them. "Send me your resume." they say.

Don't you know they say that because they don't know what else to say? You've just told them you're in the job search. The obvious response is "send me your resume." So you do. And then you wait. And wait. And wait. Where's that perfect job they're going to help you find? Still waiting.

Here's a better approach. Forget about the resume that nobody cares about. Never send your resume to anyone you think may be of hiring caliber. Pick up the phone and request a meeting (make sure you have a referral!) to get advice and counsel. If, after you have secured a meeting, they request your resume, go ahead and send it. If they don't request it, DO NOT send it (those kind of meetings are ALWAYS more interesting). And then during the meeting, focus on them and their background, and not you and your background.

And if you can make it meeting after meeting without discussing your resume, chances are good you're that much closer to your next position. And if you're still using that resume as a crutch, good luck! Just please don't send it to me!!

That being said, you're in the job search. Let's face it. You do need a resume. And if you're going to spend the time creating one, at least do it right. If you go to the bookstore, you'll find many books on resumes. And sure, some are really helpful. I just want to take you through a couple of key items that I thought were obvious, but maybe they're not.

Use Your Resume to Position Yourself to Where You Want to Be

Your resume is a positioning statement combined with your accomplishments. If your previous accomplishments don't lend themselves to what you want to do… then don't put them in there. Recently, I met with John, a Director of IT who wants his next job to be as a Chief Information Officer. As I read through John's resume, it was painfully glaring that this was not the resume of a CIO. It was the resume someone who would be an overqualified IT Manager bordering on Director.

John, get this low level information out of here. All of this where you scheduled and performed remote backup the data center. CIOs don't schedule and perform backups. They have people for that. Everything about his resume put him back to what he did five years ago. CIOs think big picture. They figure out how to assess the business and align it with technology to support the business model. Show me somewhere in your background where you did anything relative to that. The reality is that he had, but he wasn't thinking like the CIO he wanted to be. He was thinking like the Director of IT he'd already been.

How long should it be? Two pages. That's it! No more questions. Don't waste my time. If you can't fit your story on two pages, I can't hire you because I don't have time to employ someone who isn't capable of effectively taking relevant information and presenting it in a concise manner. Plus, any more than two pages, and you're telling everyone that you're very, very old.

But if you have less than five to seven years of work experience, one page will do. I've met some college grads who haven't even turned in their cap and gown manage to have two page resumes. And I just think, "You've got to be kidding me." You have practically no real work experience, and you've managed to fill up two pages with a bunch of odd jobs and class work? You're not fooling anyone!

One of the keys to a good resume is to remove the clutter, and get people to focus on what's really important. The easiest ways to get rid of clutter in your resume are:

1. Remove home address.

2. Remove college graduation dates.

3. Show dates of employment in years (not month-year).

4. Only list real degrees from real colleges. Just because you spent a week at Harvard in some leadership seminar doesn't mean that you should put Harvard on your resume. In fact, by putting it on there, you're calling out the fact that you didn't go to Harvard for college.

5. Remove certifications unless your position requires it or your degree is completely irrelevant and you need to show that you actually have some type of training for the field in which you're claiming to be an expert.

6. Remove Hobbies, Interests and the line "References Available Upon Request."

7. Remove irrelevant positions or your first few positions out of college.

8. Remove the middle initial in your name.

9. And finally, if your name is Andrew, but you go by Ted, feel free to put Ted on your resume.

Results. The bullet points in your resume should be WHAT you've accomplished. Not HOW you accomplished it. They should be statements of performance with results. I should be able to answer the question, "How much by when?" for every statement.

Here are a few ideas:

From this...	*To this...*
Sold products to retailers.	Increased sales by $150M within the first six months of new retail product launch.
Managed a team that supported company's computer network.	Managed an average of 250 customer support calls per day with a satisfaction rating of 99.8%. Implemented technology system that reduced operational costs by 35% in one year.
Managed call center operations.	Built call center from 8 seats to 250 seats within three months.

| | Decreased operational costs by 72% within first year by implementing call routing system. |
| | Reduced wait times from four minutes to 32 seconds while increasing customer satisfaction by 20%. |

Naming your resume. Let's see, there's Jane Francis MBA.doc and JaneFrancis2008.doc, JFrancisResume1a.doc, jf2vers3.doc, myresumenew.doc and probably a whole host of others. Everyone likes a little mystery, but not when it comes to the coding of your resume! I can't believe how many people send me a copy of their resume called *Resume.doc* or *Resume07a.doc*. Please, name your resume *firstlastresume* and then PDF it so your resume remains formatted the way you planned.

How Many Versions of Your Resume Do You Have?

That's a great question. And the answer is pretty clear.

But before I tell you how many, let me remind you of what it's like to hire someone. You remember, right? You remember going through resume after resume... with not one person who fit exactly what you were looking for. You have a strong engineering background. What? This is a marketing position. I can't make the leap that engineering is a good training ground for marketing – especially when so many brilliant, experienced marketing minds are out there!

You're a CFO in the Manufacturing industry? What are you doing applying for this VP of Finance position in Insurance? You dealt with widgets. We deal with taking people's money month after month with the hopes of never actually having to deliver a product or service to anyone.

61

But then, after poring through hundreds of resumes, you see it. You see the one that seems like it was written for the job! And maybe... just maybe... it was.

Because maybe, just maybe, the person you chanced upon was not only qualified, but very, very smart. And maybe that person went through the job description line by line, figured out what they did relative to each point somewhere in their past, and produced a purely customized version of their resume. And lo and behold, you have a perfect fit! (The more I think about this, the more I think it would be a great business idea! Input your resume. Input the job description. Press Blend. And out comes your personalized resume for that specific job.)

But wait, you say, is that fair? Sure. It's called positioning. Companies do it all the time. Take a look at these examples.

Fact: Unemployment rate hits 8%.

Positioning: Americans having more free time than ever.

Fact: Intel lays off 5,000 workers.

Positioning: Intel develops new process that increases company productivity by 32%.

Here's the real question you have to ask yourself: With the background, experience and skill set I have, do I truly believe that I could do the job? Do I truly believe that I'm capable of performing at the highest levels in this position? Am I truly the best person for this job? And if the answer is yes, then you need to get yourself in the game. And you can do that with your customized resume!

Do not leave it up to HR or the hiring manager to make the leap based on what you used to do. You need to be qualified based on what they want done now. They don't have time to read between the lines. You don't have time nor can you afford to leave it in their hands!

Now don't for a second think that I'm suggesting you lie. Never, never, never lie on your resume! I am suggesting, however, that you can change the wording to say essentially the same thing. Here's what some repositioning might look like:

Requirement: Experience in the pharmaceutical industry.

Your Background: Managed 15 large accounts, two of which were in the Pharma industry.

Positioning: Developed new business in the pharmaceutical industry increasing year over year sales by 50%.

While you're at it, you should figure out how to leverage that pharmaceutical industry conference/golf outing you attended – where you met (i.e., developed relationships) with more than 30 suppliers of pharma products.

Do you think the hiring managers will realize that you did this? I don't. Why? Because most people don't even take the time to change their resume. Most people are far too lazy. Most people don't even send a cover email. Most people don't even worry about the format of their resume (and by the way, most people should!). Most people just hit "apply" and send their same old generic resume – the one that's all things to no one.

So back to the original question: How many versions of a resume should you have? The answer is infinite. You should have a custom resume for every job opportunity (maybe now you'll be a little more discriminating in what you apply for!). But, won't that take a long time? Sure it will. But you know what won't take a long time? The hiring manager pressing the delete button because your background doesn't match the job description. That will be very quick. Good thing you didn't spend a lot of time on it, right?!

Thirteen Mistakes That Will Ruin Your Chances of Getting Hired by Me

When I was hiring an assistant, I became overwhelmed with the responses and appalled at some of the errors. Here are some insights based on the responses I received. If anything, it might make you feel a little bit better about yourself!

1. **You called me Sir.** Last time I checked, I was not knighted by the Queen. And more importantly, I'm not a male. Go back to your medieval castle. No, better yet… off with your head!

2. **You replied back with your resume.** That's it. Nothing else. You know what? I'm going to spend as much time on you as you did on me. You pressed Send. I'll press Delete.

3. **You sent me a .wps or .rtf file.** Hate to break it to you, but Microsoft Word is the word processor of the world. If you're not using it, it tells me that you're not up to date on technology. I can't believe you used Works to do your resume. What are you working on? A PC Junior? Do you even know what a PC Junior is?

4. **Your formatting stinks.** I can't even believe how horrible your resume looks. Different typestyles, different point sizes, the margins aren't consistent. You should have PDF'd the document so what I see is what you sent.

5. **You have a typo.** Yes, it's there. Right in the section where you tell me you have "ecxellent attention to detail."

6. **You may have made a mistake... but I can't take the risk:** "I am computer illiterate." Yikes. Thanks for sharing. Why did you even apply? Maybe the Amish are hiring.

7. **Your reason for me hiring you:** "I'm currently unemployed and need work." Well, I currently need to win the lottery, but that doesn't mean the guy pulling out the Bingo Balls is going to draw my number, does it? Give me a real reason... like what you might be able to do for me – given the job requirements.

8. **You spelled Advisor wrong.** You obviously didn't give spelling advice. And "temparary." Way to sound it out. Don't you know that the red underline means the word is spelled wrong? I'll give you temparary. Delete.

9. **You gave me too much information in the name of your document.** LizSmithCorrectedResume. Glad you corrected it... but did you have to tell me that you had an incorrect version? This one was my favorite: Moms Resume. Hey Mom... are your kids returning the favor for all of the homework you did for them in school? Are you going to have them do your job for you once you're hired as well?

10. **You gave me your My Space link.** How old are you? Twelve? I don't want to see your My Space account. I don't want to know that you even have a My Space account.

11. **Your email has the name of an animal in it.** Bunny, snow leopard, tigress. That is sooooo adorable. How can I possibly take you seriously with an email like that?

12. **You put the wrong job title in your cover letter.** Hey... I know you're applying for other positions... but at least try to make me feel a little bit special. If you're going to customize the letter, get it right.

13. **You wrote something really strange.** "I was entertained with the large variety of activities." What? Did you work for the circus? Sounds like you just sat back and watched while everyone else worked. I don't need to hire a spectator who sits on his rear all day long and is entertained. Then again, you're the same person that told me, "I self-teach and individually learn programs." Wow, you both teach yourself and learn them individually. What an accomplishment... for a Siamese twin joined at hip (Maybe you really are in the circus?). Why don't you go back to grade school and self-teach yourself some English.

Has this challenging job search caused you to lose all levels of enthusiasm? Maybe it's partially your fault. All I can say is clean up your act. If you're going to spend the time applying for positions, at least make it professional. Fix the typos. PDF the professional-looking resume. Send me a cover letter that speaks to the requirements of the position. And make yourself sound like an interesting, exciting, intelligent (and fun) person that my business absolutely can't do without.

Other Formats

Executive Summary

Some people may request an executive summary instead of a resume. This is a one-page document that lists the following (in an easy-to-read, at-a-glance format):

1. Name (cell phone, email)

2. Focus (paragraph with bullet points of strengths)

3. Professional Areas (industries, companies, key positions)

4. Key Accomplishments (five to eight bulleted lines)

5. Education & Activities (degrees, boards, honors)

Professional Bio

On the very rare occasion, some people may request a professional bio instead of a resume. This is not your resume with the word "BIO" at the top. A good bio consists of a few paragraphs of your major positions. If you need some ideas, take a look at some executive bios under the Investor Relations section of public company websites.

Don't make the mistake of sending a resume, bio and executive summary all at once. The reason you do three different ones is to respond to three different types of requests. And if you don't have a bio and executive summary, don't worry about it. Wait until someone requests something other than your resume.

Video Resumes

A new phenomenon is the video resume. This bodes well for people interviewing for positions where being filmed is appropriate.

A woman I know who does training put a few clips of her training a class on YouTube and then provided a link in her cover letter. What a great idea!

If you're not naturally comfortable in front of the camera, and your position doesn't require you to be in front of the media – or doing lots of presentations – don't bother with this. Your time would be better spent going out and meeting new people and building your network!

Molly's Takeaways

1. Use your resume to position yourself for the job you want – not the ones you've already had.
2. Make sure it's free of clutter and looks highly professional.
3. Send your resume as a PDF attached to a cover email.
4. Create a resume for each position for which you are applying.

CHAPTER 6: ELECTRONIC TOOLS

I constantly hear people talk about how much the job search has changed. How they haven't had to look for a job... ever. How everything is so different. And it's all about the Internet. Yes, the Internet has replaced the classifieds. And we're using technology more than ever. But getting a job is still about having conversations. And too many people let technology get in their way.

The Problem With Job Postings

So often, I find that people look for jobs by searching job boards. What's posted is not the universe of what's out there! When are people going to realize that? Have you ever met people who got hired for positions that you didn't even know existed? Maybe they didn't exist.

Maybe someone had an idea about a job – but didn't quite know what to do with it. And then they met you. All of a sudden, it becomes clear. You would be perfect for that project, that new market, that expansion. The one the company hadn't taken on, because it didn't have the right set of skills on board, and they didn't even know where to begin on putting together a job description.

I was having a conversation with Sharon. She was looking for work in the telecom industry, and I suggested she take a look at Verizon. "But they don't have any positions open." she told me. How did she know? Well, she really didn't. She didn't see any postings on their website, so she immediately assumed that there were no positions open. Maybe one of the positions they're trying to fill is the Website Content Manager – who keeps the site updated.

The reality is that not every company is that organized, nor are they interested in posting every position they have. Not every company follows the same policy. Not every division within every company follows the same procedure. Not every hiring manager within a division follows the rules. Why should you?

Higher-level positions typically never get posted. When was the last time you saw a posting on IBM's website for CEO or even a vice president? And you know what else doesn't get posted? The jobs that are not yet fleshed out. The ones that are figments of a manager's mind, and they're not quite sure everything the position will entail, but they know they need to fill it. They usually fill it when they serendipitously meet the right person.

People who think that job postings are the entire universe of what jobs are actually available are sorely mistaken. It's safe to say that job postings represent a surprisingly small percentage of what's actually available. And if you're spending all your time sitting in front of the computer, looking for the perfect job, then you're going to have a lot of lonely, depressing days! And you're going to miss out on a lot of opportunities.

But, there are ways to use job boards to your advantage. Here are a few of them:

- Use them for information.
- Use them to find different roles that might be interesting to you.
- Use them to see which industries are expanding.

If you find a posting you're really interested in, get a contact to that company. I once saw a great position. I figured out the company and then started working my network. I found someone who knew the head of Human Resources fairly well. I asked him to help make an introduction for me. It turned out that instead of me calling HR, HR was calling me. I ended up making the first (and second) cut without ever having an in-person meeting.

But here's what usually happens when you're hanging out with the computer. You're surfing the job boards. You find an interesting position that looks like a perfect fit. And I mean perfect. Then, you carefully word your cover letter and send it off.

And then what happens? You wait and wait and wait. Still waiting!

Quit being offended that you didn't get a reply. Get over it. If you're really interested in that company and that position, then figure out a way to network yourself into the job.

Even if a company says they're not hiring, don't believe it. There's a certain amount of attrition in every company. Really... when was the last time you heard about a company that had zero percent turnover? Aside from some government positions, it's pretty safe to say that every company of any size will need to make at least one hiring decision this year. Why not make that decision work in your favor?

Social Networking Sites

If you're not familiar with social networking tools, you might want to pull your head out of the sand, or venture out of your cave once in a while. Social networks connect you with your friends, business associates and acquaintances. They also have the ability to connect you with people you've never heard of, never met, and never want to. Before you get too deep into your networks, you may want to establish some guidelines (call them rules of engagement if you will) – about whom you'd like to have in your network.

What's great about these networks is that you're able to identify who knows whom… maybe. I say maybe because there are some people out there who appear to be playing a game of "Collect the Connections" of which the only true winners are a bunch of losers who know how to press the "Accept Invite" button. If you connect with anyone and everyone, it's obvious that your connections are not authentic. And if your connections aren't authentic, how authentic are you?

Thanks for the LinkedIn Invite... Who Are You?

I just received another one. Another LinkedIn invitation from someone, and I don't have a clue who he is. This happens a lot. I'm not certain what prompts these strangers to invite me to their network. I'm not certain why people I've barely said boo to want me in their network. I know I don't want them in mine! Maybe there's a prize for the most connections. I must've missed the memo.

Don't get me wrong. LinkedIn is a great tool. And if used with some level of responsibility and restraint, it can be very effective. But after far too many invites from complete strangers, I developed some connection guidelines (okay, rules!). I'm going to share them with you, because you just may want to develop some of your own.

1. **Did you sit in a meeting with me along with 40 other people once about three years ago (or three weeks ago)?** And with that incredible lack of one-on-one interaction you want to connect with me? I'm going to defer on this one to see if we ever actually have a meaningful conversation. Until then… No Connection For You!

2. **Did we work at the same company in a completely separate division and never ever meet ever (or go to**

the same **university)?** Terrific! I guess we have something in common. No Connection For You!

3. **Do you know someone that I know?** Congratulations. No Connection For You!

4. **Have you heard I run a group?** Great. Become an integral, meaningful part of it – assuming you fit the criteria. Until then... No Connection For You!

5. **Do you put your email address in your LinkedIn Name?** Good for you. Even if you are my friend, I don't want to connect with you. By putting your email address in your name, you're telling everyone that you'll connect with anyone. Therefore, your connections are not authentic. The other day, a friend asked for a referral to someone they found – a second degree connection from me. I checked my LinkedIn connections and figured out this person was connected to someone I know who connects with anyone. Therefore, all of his connections are suspect (including mine I guess). I would NEVER refer this person (or anyone connected to him) to anyone. No Connection for You!

6. **Have I known you for less than ninety days?** Quite possibly... No Connection For You! A while back, I developed the ninety day grace period for accepting invitations. This gives me a little more comfort that you're not some fly-by-night, one-meeting wonder.

7. **Did we just meet on an airplane and have a really interesting conversation for two hours and I think you're fascinating?** You know what? I'll probably connect with you, and hope that we sit next to each

other again one day. But until then, I know we'll stay in touch.

8. **Are you a friend of mine from school, work or church and I actually know who you are?** I'd love to reconnect with you. And thanks to LinkedIn for making it possible!

I pride myself in being authentic. I want my LinkedIn network to reflect my level of authenticity. When someone asks me about someone in my network, I want to know this person by name and face. I want to be able to say great things about them. All of these things are possible only if I actually know the people. If I don't know you, please don't invite me into your LinkedIn network. And guess what? I'll try not to invite you to mine!

Before connecting with someone, ask yourself the following questions:

- Who is this person?
- Have I ever met them before?
- How do I know them?
- Will they post embarrassing things about my life on this site?

I met a salesperson who doesn't accept LinkedIn invites from anyone outside of his industry. He will only connect with you if you are a coworker, customer or a partner. If you went to college with him and want to connect, try his Facebook account. What's great about this strategy? It's clean. He knows exactly who you are, and he's very purposeful in his communications. All of his "status updates" have to do with some kind of impressive result – where he was able to get a customer to market faster, or reduce costs by 50 percent.

I loved his strategy. It's so diametrically opposed to those people who will connect with anyone and everyone – whose networks are not authentic.

A cautionary tale of social networks. Be careful about what your profile says about you. And remember that you don't always have complete content control. LinkedIn gives you complete control, but on other sites, like Facebook, people can "write on your wall." What others say about you is out there for everyone to see.

How do you keep that professional?

How do you ensure that you're not just hiding behind these fancy electronic tools? Most importantly, remember that sitting in front of a computer is not going to land you a job. You have to get out and have real conversations with real people.

Molly's Takeaways

1. The position you're looking for probably won't be posted online.
2. Learn to use social networking tools judiciously.
3. Every company has some degree of turnover. Make sure when an opening comes up, they think of you.
4. Meeting face-to-face is the only way to learn if that perfect position even exists.

Molly Wendell

CHAPTER 7: WORKING WITH RECRUITERS

Not a week goes by without someone asking me, "Do you know any good recruiters?" And I'll tell you there are many really great recruiters out there, and quite a few that aren't so great (just like any industry). By definition, a great recruiter is one that places YOU in a fantastic position. Now here's the challenge…

In general, recruiters are primarily interested in speaking with you if you fit 12 of the 10 criteria for a specific position. Their motivation is to deliver EXACTLY on the job specification for fear their client will fire them for not listening. So many people in the search tell me, "If I could just get to the recruiter and explain why, even though I don't meet some of the criteria, I'm still the perfect person for the job…." And I'll tell them, save your breath. You're barking up the wrong tree.

I remember Chris telling me about this position she was absolutely perfect for – in the consumer goods industry. She spoke with the recruiter, and although she came from manufacturing, she tried to convince the recruiter that marketing was marketing. This recruiter was not retained to find someone who didn't meet the specs of the job description. Quit wasting their time! More importantly, quit wasting your time!

But let's say a recruiter got your name and wants to speak with you about a position. They'll usually ask if it's a good time. Here's a tip: Tell them it's not, and reschedule for a time that is convenient for you. Ask them to send you the position. That way, you can spend a little bit of time preparing what you might say.

This was typical of my experience with most recruiters. I got a call from a recruiter named Linda. She calls me every so often. The first time she called me, she was referred to me through a friend. She proceeded to read some really long job description, inserting my name in there just a few times to make it seem personable. Then she asked me if I knew anyone that might fit. She seemed nice. I gave her about five names of people I thought she should speak with.

A month later, she called again. This time, she left a message – reiterating everything that happened on our last call, along with whom I referred. It told me one thing… she takes really great notes. But amazingly, she flails in the follow-up process – failing to mention if any of my contacts made it to the interview process. She then began to read what sounded like a really long job description. I'm not really sure though, because I deleted the message.

A month later, she called again. I let her go to voicemail. Her message began by reminding me what happened on the first call, then… who knows what the rest of the message said, because I deleted it.

Here's why I deleted it. Two reasons. First, she somehow thinks she's doing me some favor by calling me and milking me for my contacts. I just see her as wasting my time. Secondly, I know very few people who've been placed by a recruiter. And people like her are giving the industry a bad name.

How do I recommend working with recruiters? Start working with recruiter while you still have a job. Take their calls. Help them out. Hire them. When you're looking, they might be just a little bit more indebted to you.

And if it's too late for that, remember this. Just because a person is a recruiter and you're looking for a job doesn't automatically require that they talk to you. Recruiters are just as busy as the rest of us. They're trying to deliver for their clients. They may not have the time to meet with you. They may not want to make the time to meet with you. If a recruiter is not taking your calls or answering your emails, maybe you're partially to blame.

Have you given them a good reason to want to meet with you? Did you get a great referral? Be worthy of their time, and they'll take the time.

If you've done a good job of earning the right to take up their time, be sure to get something out of it. Tap them for **their** contacts. Get some industry information. Find out what other searches they're doing. See how you can be of value to them. It's a two-way street.

One thing recruiters should know. I'm going to remember how you treated me when I was in my search. And when I land and have a hiring need, I know exactly which recruiter will get the business.

When I started looking, a friend sent me a list of recruiters. I had to call each one to learn they weren't a specialist in my field. It was a lot of calls. Now, there are tools to help you narrow down the field… to find the ones that are specialists in your specific industry or functional area.

I wonder why so many people are enthralled with recruiters. Why they want to be in such good graces with them. Because out of the millions of jobs, they might, just might, have one position? Why?

The position has already been defined. They go for the competition. They don't subscribe to the fact that the best people might be the ones that are currently available.

Go ahead and spend your time here, if you'd like. Just remember, recruiters are filling less than one percent of the positions out there. How much time are you going to devote to that one percent… at the expense of missing out on the other 99 percent of the opportunities?

Molly's Takeaways

1. Don't shop for a recruiter. Get referrals to them, and build a relationship.
2. Recruiters typically go to their client's competition for talent. If you're in the job search you may already be out of the running.
3. If a recruiter contacts you, schedule a time to talk after they've sent you the details.
4. Don't spend a large percentage of your job search in an area that fills such a small percentage of the jobs.

CHAPTER 8: JOB SEARCH MEETINGS

Every good job search includes participation in meetings that are strictly for job seekers. Why is this important? People who are in the search typically know more about who is hiring, who's not, and they learn about opportunities that may not be a fit for them, but may be for you. People who already have jobs are doing what you probably used to do: spending most of your waking hours trapped in the four walls of your office, not getting out there meeting new people, and doing a less-than-stellar job of building your network.

You'll be amazed how much information you learn about the market by going to one job search meeting. Some meetings are targeted toward a specific function or level, while others are general. Many churches have employment ministries that include job search networking meetings as well as information to help you in the search, such as resume writing and effective interviewing techniques. Professional networking groups like Executives Network (www.executivesnetwork.com) are targeted toward upper management levels. If you are not the target market for a specific type of group, don't attend. Do yourself and the group a favor by attending only those that are appropriate for your level.

What to say. A good job search meeting typically consists of a group of people sitting around a table, with each person having a turn to tell the group who they are, what they're looking for, and where they need help. Too often, a first-timer (or worse… someone who's been there a few times) says:

"My name is Jim Smith. I'm a CFO. I spent the last thirty years in the retail industry but I believe my skills are transferable. I'm open to any size company, in any industry, in any location. If anyone knows of any place that can use me, please let me know."

Yes, I know a place. It's called Vagueville! And they're not hiring! This person has basically told the group, "I am completely unprepared for one of the most important decisions in my life. I have no idea where I want to work and I'm leaving my options up to a bunch of strangers who barely know me."

Do everyone a favor (including you) and get prepared for your search. You may find that your focus changes over time, but at least start with something. It's very difficult to help someone who doesn't know how to help themselves. A prepared job seeker says something like this:

"My name is John Smith. I'm a CFO having spent my last assignments in the telecom industry with Nortel Networks and AT&T. I am looking for a lead finance position for a medium or large company (state employee or revenue size) or possibly a venture-backed startup in the telecom or technology industries. My preference is Denver, but I'm also interested in commuting to California. Specifically, I'm looking for contacts with Verizon Wireless, Alltel, Virgin Mobile, and any venture capital firms focused on wireless or telecom."

And then, wait for others to give you contacts. If the well is dry, you may want to have some backup ideas or list a few more companies (but don't be the person who lists 15. By the time you've read off the seventh one, we've forgotten the first six!).

So, you've come prepared. You've given your spiel. And lo and behold, people actually give you contacts with which to follow up. Be sure to take good notes. Write down the name, company and any contact information (email, phone). Also write down who referred you so you can reference that person when you follow up with the contact. Remember, a referred contact will typically respond faster than one in which you don't have a referral.

And if you don't feel like you're getting much help, either you're being too vague... or perhaps it's just a reminder that you need to be more helpful to others. If you can assist four or five people in their search, they're more likely to go out of their way looking for a way to help you. What comes around, goes around.

The One Thing That Might Be Standing Between You and Your Next Job

John called me. He was really excited. In an Executives Network meeting, I referred him to Brad. John wrote down the info, called Brad that afternoon and scheduled lunch for Tuesday. Midway through the lunch, Brad called his HR department and told them to call off the candidate search they were doing – because he was sitting across the table from the perfect person for the job.

How often does that happen? Someone follows up on a contact (not even a lead... just a contact), and they get a job. It happens more often than you think. And you know what happens when you don't follow up. Nothing. That's right. Absolutely nothing. How many jobs have you lost out on because you weren't diligent in your follow up? I guess you'll never know.

I'm amazed at the number of people who don't follow up. I mean really great contacts that could help them in their search. How do I know they don't follow up? Oh, I know alright! I can even figure out during a meeting who will follow up and who won't.

But we're all probably guilty of it... this lack of follow up. When I was in the job search, I definitely was. But, if I were to do it over again, that's the one thing I would do differently. I would be diligent about following up on every contact, every lead, every neighbor... everyone! It wouldn't matter who they were. Because what really matters is who they know. Even after I landed, I wished that I had made just a few more connections – realizing that they might've been helpful in my new position. But calling them now would make it look like I was trying to sell them something. And when that job wasn't all that I'd imagined, I wished I had built those other relationships to fall back on.

I've been accused of being a teacher, a taskmaster, a drill sergeant, and probably a few other names that don't bear mentioning. All because I'm adamant that people write down the referrals. It's not that I don't trust that you'll remember it... well, actually who are we kidding? That's exactly what it is. I don't trust that you'll remember it – especially after you leave the meeting, run into a friend at the coffee shop, and sit down for a few minutes. A glance at your watch tells you you're late to pick up your daughter, and you still need to run by the grocery store. By the time you get home, your wife is wondering what took so long. So do I think you're going to remember it? No, I don't. Case closed.

But here's what else happens when someone gives you a contact and you don't write it down. It looks like you're not listening. It looks like you don't think it's a valuable contact. Basically, you just dismissed the person who was trying to help you. You made them feel like their contact wasn't good enough for you. You completely and blatantly disregarded their helpful advice. Do you think they're going to help you out again?

But wait, you say, "I have a really good memory." So do I, but I at least give people the courtesy of showing them I value them. Showing them their idea/contact/referral was very important, and I want to remember it. I'm going to memorialize it on my handy little note card (probably a NetNote). And I'm going to follow up. It may not be today, but I will follow up. And then after I do, I'm going to let them know by giving them a quick call, or sending an email. I'm going to thank them for the referral and find one or two things of value I got out of it (which may even be an introduction to someone else, or better yet, a job!). And I'm going to get back to them and close that loop.

Do I always do this perfectly? No, but I sure try. And so should you. Because that referral might be the person standing between you and your next job. And if you never follow up, you'll never know.

Getting Referrals

What if you're targeting a company and don't have a referral? Get one. Ask everyone you know (and meet) if they know anyone at the company you're looking at. Talk to people who are customers, partners, or suppliers to the company. Talk to people in the same industry, and see if any competitors know people there. Did you recently see an article in the paper about the company? Ask the reporter for a contact (be sure to tell the reporter what a great article it was!). Check Linkedin.com for people in your network who know people at that company. If you really want to get a contact at a company, you can. Sometimes you just need to be a little creative.

And when you think referrals, there's no such thing as too many!

Thanks but I already have a contact. When I sit in the Executives Network meetings, I listen to people offer up a contact, only to have the person on the receiving end say, "Thanks, but I already have a contact at that company." That's just great. That 10,000 plus person company, and you have one contact. Congratulations! Here's a needle. There's a haystack. Go for it!

Or how about this approach? If you really want to target a company, why don't you meet as many people in as many different departments as possible and learn as much as you can about each area? When I was targeting commercial real estate, I met with six different people at the same company (and the office only had 15 people total). You think I didn't know virtually everything going on? Some people probably thought I worked there already! Another benefit of meeting with all of those people is that I realized I absolutely would not be a fit at this organization, but that didn't become apparent until I was meeting with person number five.

Here's an idea: If someone offers up a contact, you say thank you! And follow up! You never know who else that person might know. And you can now tap into their network and expand your possibilities.

Why would someone I don't even know help me in my job search? Good question. Let me ask you something. If you had the opportunity to help someone, would you? Of course you would. Guess what? So would just about everyone else. Just because someone doesn't know you doesn't mean they won't help you. How many people have you opened a door for – without ever introducing yourself? How many times have you done something nice for someone without ever expecting them to return the favor? I'd like to go on record right now and thank everyone on the airplane who has ever helped me put my luggage in the overhead compartment. What do I pack? Rocks?

We live in a helpful society. Sometimes it's more helpful than we want it to be. But when it comes to job search, if someone who's out of work has the ability to help a fellow job seeker, it makes them feel good. It brings them joy. Please don't deny a person the opportunity to have joy! It might be the only joy they have all day!

The Strength of the Weak

There's a unique phenomenon about the job search – first discussed in the '70s by influential sociologist, Mark Granovetter. It's called "The Strength of the Weak." It's about the strength of your connections. This concept suggests that the people you know the least will help the most. And in turn, the people you know the most will help you the least. After all, if your friends knew about a position, wouldn't they have told you already? Most people I know begin their job search with their family and friends. I say forget the family and friends. They can love you and support you, but when it comes to effective job search, by and large, they are basically useless!

If your weak connections will give you the strongest referrals, who should you be spending your time with? Begin spending more time with people you barely know, and you'll get more solid contacts than you ever thought possible!

Remember this phenomenon of the strength of the weak even when you have a great network. You'll probably hear about more opportunities than those who don't. But, when you need that network to work for you, you might find yourself starting over – building a new network to help you for today. And when you're looking again in a few years, you'll need to build another network. The bottom line is that you can't stop building your network!

Molly's Takeaways

1. Go to every job search meeting prepared to talk about your background, what makes you different and desired position.
2. Accept, record, and follow up on every contact and lead you get.
3. Don't forget your manners. A call or email to thank someone for a referral (even a dead end) opens the door a little wider for the future.
4. The more new connections you have in your network, the more solid and effective it becomes for your job search today.

Molly Wendell

CHAPTER 9: NETWORKING EVENTS

To build your network and maximize your opportunities, it is critical that, in addition to attending job search meetings, you attend a fair amount of networking events. How many? When I was in the search, I'd go to about 10 to 15 per week. That seems like a lot. But, I was serious about my job search. And I was serious about building a network. I'd already spent one solid year hanging out in front of the computer – getting lonely and depressed – and I realized the only way I was going to make connections and find the right opportunity was to get out and meet people.

How do you find the events? Basically, on any given day, open the newspaper and see what's happening. You can bet there will be a breakfast meeting, lunch meeting and/or dinner/happy hour virtually every night of the week.

With so many out there, which ones should you attend? You'll want to have a good balance of all types. Go to industry events – especially those in your target industries. Go to functional area events – of your functional area as well as others. As a marketing professional, I'd often go to finance-type events. It was great because I had no competition in the room and stood out from the crowd. Go to other business events in your community that will attract people from all industries and functional areas.

Test out a few and see if you're meeting the type of people you'd like. Typically, you don't have to be a member of the organizations to attend the events. And don't forget the charity events… because they're everywhere!

You might not think it's that important, but let's talk about your nametag. When you put on a nametag at any event, put your first and last name. How many times have you been to an event to see Bob on a nametag… and that's it? Who does he think he is?

Cher? Madonna? And wear your nametag on your right side (the side opposite your heart). Why do you do this? When shaking hands, it provides a line of sight to your name, and people will be more likely to remember it. Unless you just put Bob... and in that case, who cares where you wear it!

Types of Events

Depending on whether you're a morning person or a night person, you'll probably gravitate toward certain types of events.

Typically, morning events are breakfast meetings. You'll have a brief amount of time to network before and after breakfast, but not during. These events are great if you're uncomfortable working a room. The key here is to utilize the time before and after to meet people. Arrive early, and don't rush off right after the breakfast. Some of the best connections can be made lingering after the meeting.

Evening events tend to be more of a social setting, and you tend to have the opportunity to meet more people.

Regardless of which you prefer, be sure to attend a combination of both types. Morning events are not better than evening ones. Evening are not better than morning ones. If you make one quality connection, you should consider the event a success.

Don't Confuse a Networking Event With a Job Search Meeting: Act Accordingly

Too many times, people in the job search go to every function regardless of type and act like it's a job search meeting. It goes something like this, "Hi, I'm Dave Smith. I'm a CFO but I'm currently in the job search. My last company laid me off after fifteen years. I've been looking for six months now. So if you know anyone looking for a CFO, here is my card." Hey smooth talker. Don't wait by the phone, that call is NEVER coming!

Here's what happens when you tell people you're in the job search. They take pity on you and think you're going to ask them for a job. They immediately get uncomfortable, as though unemployment might be contagious, and look for some way to make a quick getaway. In reality, you're not looking for a pity party – nor is your job search contagious. You're looking for contacts that will lead you to the next opportunity. So, don't give them an opportunity to take pity on you, or make a quick getaway.

What if you did something crazy… like not tell them you're in a job search? And I don't mean make something up (like I'm a consultant – which NOBODY believes anyway – even if you are one). What if you just deflected the, "What do you do?" question to something like this?

"I'm in finance. Mike, tell me more about that trip you just took. It sounds fascinating!"

Try turning the conversation back to focusing on them as quickly as possible. And then ask question after question. Don't give them an opportunity to take pity on you. Give yourself an opportunity to have a real conversation and create a connection, maybe even make a new friend.

"But… what if they ask where I work?" you say. No problem. Don't tell them (because you don't work anywhere anyway). Just avoid the question. There's no such thing as the Networking Police (actually, maybe that's me!). No one is going to arrest you for not answering a question. I do it all the time, and no one even notices.

If you don't believe me, then why don't you try it yourself? The next time you're at a function and someone asks you a question, just change the subject. Maybe something like this:

Sam: "Molly, where do you work?"

Molly: (pause) "Hey Sam, where do you work?"

Now, this is a little difficult to get the point across in written form. (I really need to start my video blogs!) It's not confrontational. It's very casual – the pause, the look – like I'm thinking deeply as they ask me a question. So it's quite possible in their mind that I didn't even hear their question, then the, "Hey Sam, where do you work?" just comes out. Then I immediately follow it up with another question. After that, another question… the key is to not give them a chance to ask you a question.

The second they ask you a question (which means you paused too long between questions – you need to get better at not letting those pauses linger), just don't answer. Ask them something else instead. If, after a while, you've found out a lot about them and you think it's your turn to talk… you're sorely mistaken! (By the way, I used this same technique during interviews… and was offered a job more than 90 percent of the time.)

Why is it important to ask all of the questions? The more people talk about themselves, the more they'll like you. The more they like you, the more they'll open up their network to you… which just might be where you find your next job.

You can either scare people away, or you can engage them. It's your choice.

Structured Events

If you're attending structured events such as dinners, lunches, and breakfast meetings, be prepared with good table conversation. Scan the newspaper and local business journal to get up to date on current events. Read *Fortune* magazine. It has great articles about many different industries. Whether you're into entertainment or not, realize that many others are. *People* magazine or *Us Weekly* will let you know who's with whom, who's not, and the latest in all the celebrity gossip.

I once ran a seminar where some guy in the back of the room, arms crossed, obviously not buying into this concept, said, "I would NEVER read *People* magazine, and I don't believe that will help me in any way get a job." (Maybe your lousy attitude and inability to be open to new ideas might be the problem?)

All he wanted to do was talk about golf. That's fine if everyone he meets wants to talk about golf. But he's forgetting the number one rule of networking that so many people forget. It's not about you. It's about them. It's not about what you're interested in. It's about what they're interested in. If you want to spend the rest of your life only talking about your interests, you're going to have a tough time building a great network.

What about sports? Any big tournaments or events happening? This is a rhetorical question... because there's always some type of sporting event that just happened or is about to happen! ESPN SportsCenter will get you up to speed.

And while you may not be a huge fan of television, just remember, a lot of people are! If you haven't tuned in at least once to some of the top shows, you should. Because it's not about you talking about your favorites, it's about you asking smart questions. Not sure what's popular? Ask a few friends what they watch (or just read the entertainment section of your local newspaper).

I once went to a breakfast meeting (how I loathe the breakfast meeting!) where the entire table conversation was dominated by two people talking about their hometown. I was stuck in the middle of an ad hoc reunion that wasn't ending any time soon! I thought about moving to a different table, but it would've looked rude. I vowed to never get stuck at a boring table again. From then on, I approach set tables with the question, "Are you the fun table?" If they say yes, I sit down. If they just look at me questioningly, I know immediately that they're not, in fact, the fun table... and save myself from being stuck!

Once you sit down, be sure to introduce yourself to each person at the table. And if there's no conversation going, you may want to get it started with some broad questions about something current. And you know what's current, because you did your homework (i.e., read the newspaper and *People* magazine and watched SportsCenter).

About The Speaker

After the event, there's typically a crowd around the speaker. Maybe it was someone you wanted to meet. Next time, don't just approach the speaker on your own... because anyone can do that. Instead, find someone who knows the speaker (perhaps someone at the table you were at?), and ask for an introduction. Then, approach the speaker and let that person "introduce you" to the speaker. Automatically, your credibility will be enhanced because you had a "referral" in!

So... now you know the speaker and you're just standing there. Oftentimes, I'll see people hand the speaker their card (like they wanted it?) and tell them how great they are. What do you expect the speaker to do next? Quit making life awkward for all of us, and try this. Compliment the speaker and then immediately ask a question or present a statement (with questions attached) to engage the speaker in relevant conversation. The key is to get the conversation started... not stopped!

This assumes that you want to build a relationship with the speaker. If you don't, then there's no need to introduce yourself.

Unstructured Events

Unstructured events are typically happy hours or social functions that take place in the evening. If you're not comfortable walking into an event that's already started, then you might want to get there early.

Once, I went to an event early (trust me, it was purely accidental). There was only one other person there. So we had to talk to each other. The next person who walked in did what? Yes, he joined us. The next person after that? You guessed it. She joined us too. They had to because we WERE the party. What happens when you get there early is that you're the nucleus of the party and the party builds around you. Eventually, like any positive charge, you break off and go speak with others, but at least you now have your "friends from the beginning" that you can always go back to.

One of my favorite things to do is stand by the door and welcome everyone who comes in. "Hello! Great to see you! So glad you could make it." They remember me for two reasons. First, they were excited to have someone who was "glad they made it." Second, they think I'm the host running the event. The combination of these might give them just a little more incentive to remember me.

How to Approach a Group

So, you're at the event, moving from group to group. What's the easiest way to approach a new group of people you haven't met? Simply join them and say, "I don't believe we've met. I'm Susan Jones." And then get their names. You obviously never want to interrupt someone who's talking, so wait for an opening.

I've seen many people join a group, interrupt the conversation to introduce themselves, and immediately start taking over the conversation. It only takes a few minutes before people from the group start leaving! Remember, you're a guest to the group... so wait your turn.

The good networker is always prepared to ask great questions to get the others talking. You're asking questions to gauge interests and determine if you might be able to make a good connection. After asking questions for a couple of minutes, if you haven't found a connection, then you're either asking the wrong questions, or there isn't a connection. Before you decide that the problem is in the connection, just know that in all my years of networking, I've met very few, if any, people with whom I haven't found some sort of connection or common ground. Which then leads me to... you're probably not asking the right questions.

Good Questions to Ask

Too often, I find that people don't really know how to open a conversation, and they start with something stupid like, "How's business?" That opening line takes about as much forethought as, "Nice weather we're having." Let's take it one step further, and see what that conversation looks like:

Jim: *"Hello Bill, how's business?"*

Bill: *"Fine. Thanks."*

Jim: *"Great."*

(long, uncomfortable pause)

Jim: *"Catch up with you later."*

Bill: *(under his breath) "Don't bother Mr. Conversation Killer!"*

Do everyone a favor, and think before you speak! Ask interesting questions that will start conversations, not stop them!

What makes a great question is the potential for follow-up to identify connections or common ground. Here's an example:

Where do you work?

"Hello, I'm Bill Smith."

"Nice to meet you Bill. I'm John Jones."

"So John, where do you work?"

"I work for the Mayo Clinic."

"Wow, how long have you been there?"

"Going on two years now."

"Oh, where were you before?"

"I was with IBM."

"Sounds like you must've moved here from Rochester, Minnesota?"

"Actually I did. How did you know that?"

"Well, I'm from Minnesota (common ground) and the only two companies in Rochester are Mayo and IBM! So that seems like an interesting transition? What brought you to Mayo from IBM?"

"Mayo wanted to integrate some new technology that I specialize in."

"Interesting, my background is technology too (common ground). What kind of technology?"

You get the picture. Notice that even though Bill was also from Minnesota, he didn't start talking all about himself, but kept the conversation on John?

Maybe you didn't live in Minnesota, and maybe you're not in technology, but perhaps you know someone who works at Mayo or IBM, and even though they're big companies, you never know if they might know each other.

Let's try another one:

What do you do?

"Hello, I'm Sue Smith."

"Nice to meet you Sue, I'm Jan Dovers."

"Jan, what do you do?"

"I'm an executive recruiter." (good one!)

"Wow, how long have you been a recruiter?"

"Actually just a few years. Before this I worked in HR for JP Morgan Chase."

"Interesting, I used to work for Bank One (common ground). So, what made you make the switch?"

"Well, I used to do a lot of high-level recruiting for the new branches we opened, and decided that it was my favorite part of the job. When DHR International approached me about joining them, I thought it was an easy decision."

"Oh, I know a few folks from DHR. Do you know (name)?"

Remember that very few people work for the same company they did a few years ago. Very few people are doing the same role that they were initially trained in/got their degree in. Very few people live in the same place they were born. And even if they're living in the same state, chances are good that they moved somewhere else for a while.

These conversations are probably not the most fascinating, but they're buying you time (and earning you the right) to get a little more personal, and potentially build the foundation of a relationship.

Bad Questions to Ask

"How's business?" This is bad because only two possible answers exist and both stop the conversation.

"Lousy, and that's why I'm here at this function, trying to network and build my business!" And this is where the conversation stops.

"Great." and this is where the conversation stops.

"What do you think of the weather?" Everyone knows that when someone brings up the topic of the weather, the conversation is so boring, there's nothing left to say. At that point, you may be better served to excuse yourself and find someone interesting.

Sometimes questions are just too personal to ask and are probably not the best to open a conversation.

"Are you married?"

"No."

"Do you have kids?"

"No."

"What about pets?"

"No."

Three strikes. YOU'RE OUT!

What If I've Met Someone Before and They Act Like They Don't Remember Me?

First, get over yourself. Second, they probably don't remember you. Third, adopt the strategy to always introduce yourself with your first AND last name when you meet people. If you've met them before but are unsure whether they remember you, then go ahead and say, "Hi Bill, I'm Tom Smith. We met at (name location). Great to see you again!"

Most people are not good at remembering names, yet they get offended when others don't remember their name! Again, get over yourself. Once you're certain they know who you are (and you're certain because they said your name before you said theirs), then it's safe to quit with the first/last name greeting. But until then, keep doing it.

What if you've already met someone a few times and they still don't remember you? Again, get over yourself. I once met a man five times before he finally remembered who I was. Did it bother me? Not really. Apparently, the other four times, I must not have made much of an impression (even though one of the times was a two-hour, one-on-one job interview where I was offered – but declined – the job). So what? Does he know who I am now? Yes.

Here's My Card. Uhhh, No Thanks!

When do we exchange business cards? That depends. My theory on business cards is that you want to get them, not give them. If you're speaking with someone and they seem interesting, and you'd like to set up a time to meet with them, then say, "I'd love to talk more about this. Let me get your card and I'll follow up with you." Do you give your card to them? No, not unless they ask for it.

I was in a taxi and the driver was sharing some incredible insight he read in a networking book. It said: Give your business card to every person you meet and tell them if there's any way you can help them, to give you a call.

I find so much wrong with this concept that I almost don't know where to begin!

First, if I meet you and you immediately hand me your card, I've got news for you. You haven't earned the right to take up real estate in my purse. And as every woman knows, that's some of the most valuable real estate around! Don't ever hand me your card until you've earned the right (and by earning the right, I mean I specifically asked for your card).

Second, it's not my job to figure out how you can help me. That's your job. If you can't figure out how to help me, then how much value are you to me? That's like going to the doctor and saying, "My back hurts." And the doctor gives you a card and tells you to call and schedule another appointment once you've figured out exactly how to fix it. Who would go back to that doctor?

And some of you may be saying, "Why would I want to figure out how to help you?" Well, right back at you! Every person I meet, I'm trying to figure out how to help them (and in case you don't know it yet, it's that — and not the number of people you know —

101

that's makes you a great networker!). Sometimes I figure out a way – other times, not so much. But it's okay, because my intent is that I can help virtually everyone I meet. If I hit 50 percent of that goal, that's not half bad (or is it half good?).

Quit thinking that the more cards you hand out, the better you are at networking. Better yet, forget about giving your card out at all. Focus more on earning the right to take the relationship to another level by figuring out how to help someone, and then act on it. The smart ones will most certainly ask for your card.

What if they have a lead for me? Should I give them my card then? ABSOLUTELY NOT! If they have a lead or contact for you, you should say, "Great, do you have a card?" Get theirs and then you can control the communication.

I met a woman who told me about a great lead from the person she sat next to on an airplane. Then she said, "I hope he calls me." She gave him her card, but didn't get any contact information from him (he was out of cards... which goes back to ALWAYS carry paper and pen with you!). Now, this great lead is at the mercy of someone else's time frame and memory. How many times have you lost someone's card? Guess what. They've lost yours as well!

What If You Get Stuck?

You're at a networking function talking with one person and the conversation is not really going anywhere. What do you do? If you've decided you need to move on, here are a couple things to do. But first, here's what NOT to do.

DON'T say to the person, "Nice talking to you." Or, "Well, you're here to meet people and I am too. Thanks for your time." Or, "I have to go to the restroom." And then leave them standing alone! Nothing is worse than being left all alone at a networking function. Nothing cries out "Inconsiderate Networking Rookie" more than the person who leaves someone standing all alone.

DO… one of the following:

Wait until someone joins your group, make the introductions, and then while they're engaged in conversation, quietly excuse yourself.

If no one is around to save you, then you'll need to get a little creative. Say something like:

> *"I'm hungry. Do you want to get something from the buffet?"*

> *"Come on, let's go meet some more people."*

And offer to bring them with you to meet others. If they leave you at that point, fine. Remember, get over it. It's not about you. But never leave someone else. I used to attend a monthly networking function and Tricia, a colleague, would stick by my side the entire night. After a while, I finally realized that her intention wasn't to speak with me the entire night. She was less comfortable with networking and knew that I would meet others and introduce her. Once I figured that out, she met more people. And so did I!

Are You Getting the Most out of Every Networking Event?

I was at a Happy Hour in San Francisco. It was really great! What made it so great was the interesting conversation. Conversation that only benefited those in the room. And that got me thinking. How many conversations are you missing because you're not in the room?

Here's the thing. Being in the room makes you step up your game. If you're sitting at home, hanging out online – sending emails

– and "networking" electronically, it's real easy to get lazy. To let your professionalism slide just a bit. After all, the dog doesn't care if you ever change out of your pajamas. But stepping out into the world (and I mean physically) gives you the opportunity have the personal interaction that humans so desperately need. If there's one thing our society is losing – it's the personal, face-to-face, one-on-one interaction. The kind where you can practice your conversational skills, test your ability to listen, read the non-verbal cues, take conversations to new directions, and see how interested AND interesting you and your peers really are.

Getting out there will force you to bring your "A" game. Step up your professionalism. Give you the opportunity to become a better conversationalist.

And if you're going to actually attend something, make a commitment to be there. And I mean really be there. How many conversations are you missing because you stop by for just a few minutes? Forget about LIFO and FIFO. You know, Last In First Out and First In First Out. This works great when dealing with inventory, but when it comes to networking, try practicing a new method. It's called FILO. First In Last Out. Go early. Stay late. If you're going to attend an event, you might as well take full advantage of it. Maximize your opportunity to meet as many people as you can. Have as many interesting conversations as possible. If you're only there for an hour, you might have three, twenty-minute conversations. But what if you stayed an extra hour? Maybe you could meet twice as many people and have twice as many interesting conversations.

Don't Forget About the Impressions You're Giving

If you're wearing your Bluetooth headset, take it off prior to walking in. It makes you look preoccupied. It makes it look like you're just waiting for some random call to rescue you. Plus, that blue, blinking light is REALLY distracting.

If you're negative, you're not interesting. Be happy, be positive. Be excited about the possibility that you might meet someone new, learn something fascinating about them, have something in common. Jobs come and go. Friendships can last forever.

If you're always talking about work or the fact that you're out of work, you're really kind of boring. I used to be in an industry where, at every event, everyone talked about the same thing – the industry. They always asked the same intro question, "How's business?" One of two answers work for that question. Good or bad. Once you got that out of the way, there just wasn't much left to talk about. The events were painful.

Focus on getting to know someone personally. Where they're from. What they like to do. Things they're involved in. Build a relationship, and see where it goes. You might make a new friend!

So get out there. Bring your "A" game. Engage in interesting, meaningful conversation. Ask smart questions. Make new friends. And stop letting the conversations go on without you!

Molly's Takeaways

1. A networking event is not the same thing as a job search meeting.
2. Be prepared to lead the conversation. Talk about things other people are interested in and ask lots of good questions. Avoid conversation-killing questions.
3. Be prepared to collect information. Bring a pen and paper and if someone has a lead for you, get their contact information so you have control and you can follow up with them.
4. This is your chance to shine. Dress appropriately. Don't be boring or negative.

Molly Wendell

CHAPTER 10: GETTING A MEETING

Just One Word to Say About Cold Calling

Don't! Just don't! Be very un-Nike-like. Don't do it! Here's what people are thinking when the phone rings. Mentally, they're saying, "Who is this and why are you wasting my time?" It may carry a little different tone when they say hello. Then again, it may not. Think quick, because that's what it's going to take to give them a good reason to stay on the phone for five more seconds. And, "I'm in the job search" is not a good reason.

Why put yourself in that position? Why not earn credibility from the start? Instead of cold calling someone, get a referral to that person. That alone should buy you the extra seconds you need to get what you want out of the call.

Learn from my friend, David. He told me about a great position he was hoping to get. It had his name written all over it, and he was very excited about it. With a little research, David figured out he and Jeff, the hiring manager, went to the same graduate school. Instead of getting a referral, David thought knowing the same fight song of their alma mater would be enough. Little did he know… it wouldn't even be close.

David made the call, immediately referenced the fact they went to the same school, and hoped for the best. What happened was the worst. Jeff answered the phone, obviously bothered by the interruption. (If he was so busy, why did he answer?) David tried to make small talk about the school, and then bring up the position. Jeff immediately, for whatever reason, decided David wasn't a fit for the position, and ended the call. That quickly. Game over.

What could David have done differently? First and foremost, David could've found someone that knew Jeff, either through a work or school connection. Then, the call would've sounded something like this: "Jeff, my name is David and I was referred to you by Bill Schulz. Bill really thinks the world of you and suggested we meet. When might be a good time?"

Right now, Jeff is feeling pretty good about himself because Bill said something nice about him. His attitude is positive. He's more open to a discussion. And, because the call was focused on a meeting that was Bill's idea, Jeff is more likely to make some time.

In all my years of being in the job search (and believe me, there have been plenty!), I've had only one person that wouldn't meet with me – at least initially. It was even a referral. I called Mike, used my reference, Becky, and suggested a meeting. Mike told me he didn't have time. I called Becky and told her. She told me to call Mike back and tell him that she said he HAD to meet with me. So I did. Amazing how quickly his schedule freed up. Mike and I met the following week.

When you're in the job search, quit thinking that placing a call to someone is enough to keep them on the phone. Instead, get a referral. Turn that cold call into a warm call. Get a meeting. Now is the time to be very Nike-like. Just do it!

Getting a Meeting With Someone.

It's easy. Get a referral.

If you've been doing your networking and you're out meeting people, you should have a target list of people you want to meet.

Wherever you are, bring your list along, and ask others if they know anyone. But please, keep your list limited to three to five people. One time I met with someone who had a list of 30 people on page one... then I realized there were five pages of this. My first thought was, "Wow, you want to meet everyone." My second thought was, "You're really unfocused!"

When speaking with others about whom you want to meet, again remember what my sixth grade English teacher taught me. "To be specific is terrific. To be vague is the plague." Don't say, "Do you know anyone that I should meet?" Figure out what industry they're from. What companies they worked for. And ask to be referred to people that are likely in their network.

A Referral Versus an Introduction. Which is Better?

My friend Alex told me he was very excited because about two weeks ago, he spoke with an ex-colleague and that person was going to make an introduction to a CEO. I said that's great. When? Two weeks ago? That may not seem like a long time when you're working, but life in the job search is a lot like dog years, and two weeks seems more like two months (or even two years). I asked Alex what he was waiting for, and he told me that his friend would get back to him as soon as he had a chance to make the introduction.

This was Alex's best lead for a position. And he just put all of the control and ownership into someone else's hands (and more importantly, on someone else's time line). And he doesn't want to pester his friend too much for fear that he'll lose the introduction (and yes, that can happen!).

What should he have done? Instead of getting an introduction, Alex might have better positioned himself with a referral. What's the difference? An introduction is when someone does just that. "Introduces" you to someone... and controls the conversation by controlling your ability to connect with a contact. A referral is when you get someone's name from a friend or acquaintance, and you control the conversation by owning the follow up. What if they don't give you the person's phone number? Big deal! Ask where the person works, and pick up the phone and call their office.

I'm sure Alex's friend would have been fine with letting Alex control the follow up. If for some reason, your friend is a complete control freak and really really, really wants to make the introduction, then take this approach. Tell them you appreciate it, and you'll plan to follow up directly with the referral by (name a date that is within five business days). Therefore, if they haven't had time to control the introduction, you're not stuck in a position of wasting your precious dog years.

How to Get A Meeting With Anyone

You've done your homework. You know with whom you'd like to meet. You even have a referral to that person (again, and if you don't, get one!). Now what do you do?

Well, here's what you **don't** do. You don't try to meet with them via email. So often, I ask people if they've connected with one of their networking targets, and they say, "I sent an email. I haven't heard back." Do you realize how easy it is to hide behind email? Of course you do… you're probably guilty of it yourself.

Instead of hiding behind your mysterious email veil, do something really crazy. Pick up the phone. You remember what a phone is, right? It's that ringing thing you answer anytime, anywhere (which is a completely separate discussion altogether!). That's right. Make Bell proud. Pick up the phone and call that person. But be strategic. I typically use the call/call/email approach. Here's what it looks like.

Make the first call when you don't believe they'll be there. I'm going to assume you're calling someone's office, so call sometime between 6 and 8 p.m. Leave a message like this:

"Hi Bill, this is Molly Wendell. Curt Fletcher suggested I give you a call and set up a time to meet. Curt said some great things about you and I'm really looking forward to meeting you. I can be reached at 415-123-4567. Again, my number is 415-123-4567. Thank you."

WARNING! Bill may actually pick up the phone, so be prepared. I remember I was getting out of a meeting one day and my phone rang. It was someone I had met at the meeting about an hour before. I picked up the call, and the person said, "Oh, I was expecting to get your voicemail."

So, I said, "Great. Let me help you with that." And I hung up. He called back and got my voicemail, just like he wanted. Right?

Okay, back to Bill. After this first message, will Bill call you back? Probably not. So, you call again – maybe three days later. This time, you call at a time when you believe Bill will be in the office. This call sounds something like this:

"Hi Bill. Molly Wendell again, referred by Curt Fletcher. I'm really looking forward to setting up a time to meet with you. Tell you what. I'm going to send you an email with some possible dates and times. If it's easier to get back to me that way, then great. Otherwise, I can be reached at 415-123-4567. Again, 415-123-4567."

Then, you've prepped them that you're going to send an email right away. I assume that if you're smart enough to dial a phone, you can probably figure out how to get someone's email. Calling the company and asking, or checking online and looking at how other people's emails are structured would be two easy ways. This is what your email looks like:

SUBJECT: Ref'd by Curt Fletcher

Bill,

I'm really looking forward to getting a few minutes of your time. Curt said so many great things about you. Please let me know if any of these work for you: Tues., 11/25 or Wed., 11/26 – anytime after 10 a.m.

Thank you,
Molly Wendell
415-123-4567

And you know what? Chances are good that Bill will respond. And if he doesn't in a timely manner (timely being about two to three weeks), I would go back to Curt and ask for his help in gently reminding Bill about me. The meeting may be further out on the calendar than you want, but that's okay. Just as long as you secure a meeting. Remember, Curt didn't give me Bill's info because he DIDN'T want a meeting to happen.

ANOTHER WARNING! If they offer to have the conversation over the phone, simply say, "Oh, I'd much rather meet in person. When's a good time?" DO NOT meet people over the phone unless you live across the country. And even then, if there's ever a way to meet in person, take that option. Even if it means it will be six months out! You'll make more progress in person than over the phone.

Don't necessarily include your resume in your follow up email confirming date, time and location. Remember, it's a networking meeting, not an interview!

And always leave a message AND a phone number! I often receive messages from people who don't leave their contact information. Sometimes people don't even leave a message because they're waiting to get me live. And more often than not, I just missed the call and could've returned it right away. BUT… I can't now because they didn't leave a number (or they didn't leave a message!). The reality is that I will give them more focused time and attention when I can talk to them on my schedule, versus them trying to reach me on theirs!

Getting a meeting is that easy. I've employed this strategy for every meeting I've ever wanted. And I've met with hundreds of people (maybe even thousands at this point). Believe me – it works. And it's a lot more effective and a lot less frustrating than waiting for an email response that's never going to show up!

Let me take you through a few networking pitfalls. Knowing what to do… and what not to do… could make or break you!

Networking Pitfall: The Referral Inquisition

Nothing's worse than giving a referral, and then getting the equivalent of the Spanish Inquisition as to the strategy of how they should approach this person. A while ago, I received a call from Steve. Steve had a friend who wanted to speak with someone at Cushman & Wakefield. He called me because he knew I used to work there. After understanding which group he wanted to talk to, I gave him the contact information for a guy named Jeff. About two months later, I got a call from Steve wanting to "know the strategy of how to approach Jeff."

Strategy, I thought! What strategy? You know I used to work with him. Here's a strategy: Pick up the phone, dial his number and say, "Is Jeff there?" And quit wasting my time!

The next time someone gives you a referral, don't be high maintenance. Ask how they know each other, get their contact info, and cut the cord! Don't forget to follow up with quick note saying,

"Thank you for the referral. We met. It was great!" No need for much more.

Networking Pitfall: Being Mysterious

Nothing makes me more suspicious than the phone call that goes something like this: "Hello Molly, a friend of yours gave me your name and suggested we meet."

My first thought is that they're trying to pitch me on some multi-level marketing scheme. And if that is in fact the case, I may need to reevaluate my friends! I immediately ask which friend, and from there I'll determine whether I have time for them.

Like I said, whenever the phone rings, most busy people are thinking, "Who is this and why are they wasting my time?" Therefore, it's critical to state your name, purpose, and your referral source up front. If it's a good purpose (or better yet, a good referral), you might buy at least ten more seconds of their time

Networking Pitfall: Call Someone Mr. or Ms.

After you've graduated from college, the only appropriate time to address someone with the title Mr., Mrs., or Ms. is when you're meeting your parents' friends or the head of a country. And in the latter case, you'd use the title of president, prime minister, king/queen, raj, emperor/empress or whatever the rest of their country calls them. I can only imagine if you're hanging out in those circles, you're probably not reading this!

Quit addressing people through email, letter, or in person by anything other than their first name. And that goes for "Dear Sir or Madam." What, are we still in the eighteenth century?

Why do so many people still address others with such formality? You might say it's a sign of respect. I might suggest that it's awkward (and even more awkward when you get it wrong, like calling a single woman Mrs., or assigning the wrong gender to someone!). It creates a fictitious sense of who might be on a higher plane. The most appropriate way to show someone a sign of respect is to call them by their name. It puts you both on a level playing field. Show them you know how to be an adult who is worthy of an actual conversation!

Networking Pitfall: Offering to Take Them to Lunch

What? Why is this a pitfall? Who doesn't like lunch? Well, I like lunch, but I don't know if I like you yet. And the thought of meeting you for the first time over what may be the longest lunch ever... I think I'll take a pass.

I will, however, be glad to meet you for coffee. I will budget forty-five minutes to one hour. I don't even drink coffee, but that's beside the point. I want to meet you at Starbucks. Some of you may say that it's very noisy, but I say go where the people go. If I meet you at a Starbucks close to your office, someone you know may stop in. And now I've just gotten a possible bonus connection!

But, you say, someone agreed to go to lunch with me. That's great. Just remember, meals require a greater time commitment. And what if you realize after fifteen minutes that you're really not connecting with this person and you're done? Getting up from the table and walking out is not always the smoothest departure (trust me, I've thought about it!). Plus, figuring out who's paying can sometimes be a little uncomfortable. Should I pay? Are they going to pay? Do we split it? It's a scenario that can be avoided by not going to lunch in the first place.

Here's a hasty generalization. Men like breakfast. I'm not sure if it's because they never get a home-cooked breakfast anymore (who does that?), or that they want to shirk all family responsibility for getting the kids ready for school. "Sorry honey. I'd love to help you out, but I have a breakfast meeting. Gotta run." Maybe it's a combination? In much of my networking, men suggest breakfast. Given that I can't stand breakfast, I usually move it to coffee. It's fine. It doesn't make them not want to meet with me.

If you suggest coffee and they suggest breakfast or lunch, you can certainly take it. Just know what decision points you'll have to deal with and be prepared.

What Do You Do When Someone Won't Meet With You?

It's a rare occasion that someone won't meet with you when you have a referral. If this happens, call back the person who referred you and tell them the situation. Say, "I was really looking forward to meeting John, but he says he doesn't have time." At that point, the refer-ee (not unlike a referee!) could call John and request that he try to find some time to meet with you. If your refer-ee doesn't think of that, please feel free to suggest it. They didn't give you the referral for it to not come through. They want to help!

If you're finding that people won't meet with you despite a referral, then you're either getting referred by the wrong people (who don't carry the necessary social capital), or your approach needs revising.

You Have a Meeting. Now What?

Show up on time (or a little early), dressed appropriately.

Here's a networking tip! If you go to Starbucks, the line is significantly shorter (and often non-existent) at twenty after and ten till the hour. Instead of spending all of your networking time in line, go there at ten till the hour, get a table, get your drink and be ready when your appointment shows up. If they have to stand in line, that's fine. Join them in line or sit at the table and go through your notes one last time.

Have paper and a pen. Thank them for meeting you… and give them a little background. Very little! Then, start with the questions; how long they've been at company x, how they like it, what's going on in the industry, their business/company, issues they face. Continue with your questions until you're done. Don't worry about not telling them your life story. What you're trying to figure out is who else they interact with or know that might be beneficial for you to meet.

When they mention a company or contact you'd like to meet, ask for a referral right away. And write it down. Getting a referral within the first few minutes of meeting someone takes all of the pressure off at the end. And you can turn one networking contact into many.

If they want to give you more time, take it. Never end the meeting until you're ready. If you've run out of questions, you're ready. If you feel like you need a few more contacts, close with, "Is there anyone else you know that might have some good advice?" But if you identify future networking contacts throughout the meeting, you wouldn't even have to ask this question. If you've done a good job of engaging them in conversation, they will probably have a few contacts for you. If you haven't (and talked about yourself the entire time), they probably want to keep their friendships and don't want to subject their friends to the torture you just inflicted on them!

Networking Tip: How to Get Better Conversations by Asking Smart Questions

Don't ruin a networking opportunity by focusing so much on your job search that you forget the person you're meeting with might actually know other people in the world. The idea of networking (whether you're in the search or not) is to open the door to their network. Not close it!

Here's a great example of how it can get slammed shut pretty quickly. I gave a contact to my friend Bill. Bill is in the job search and was targeting grocery stores. I told him, "Meet with Sharon. It'll be great!" About a week later, I was talking with Bill and asked him if he had an opportunity to meet with Sharon. He said yes, but it didn't go very well. Sharon said she wasn't hiring. I could've clobbered Bill right then and there. When I gave Bill the contact to network with Sharon, it wasn't to try to get a job from her. It was to network. Find out who she knows. Learn what's going on in the industry. Instead, Bill tried to turn it into a one-way hiring discussion and Sharon wasn't interested. What a waste of a great networking contact.

Here's what I would have done if Bill had given me the referral. Instead of telling Sharon I needed a job (which is completely beside the point), I would have started off the conversation like this. "Sharon, thanks so much for taking the time to meet with me. I really appreciate it. Bill said if anyone knows about the food industry, it's you!"

And then I would have continued with questions like this:

1. How long have you worked at (company)?

2. And where were you before that? How long were you there? (Here, you're looking for other possible connections.)

3. What do you see are the biggest changes in the industry?

4. Out of all of the players, who do you think is doing some really interesting things?

5. What's changing in the way people shop for food?

6. How does that differ within demographic circles?

7. What's the next wave or trend that everyone is trying to implement?

8. Which area of the store is most profitable? What's contributing to its profitability? Which areas of the store are least profitable? Why?

9. Grocery stores are now banks, flower shops, DVD/video rentals, Starbuck's. What's next?

10. Which competitor do you think is going to lead the pack? Who's going to fall behind? What do you think are their options?

11. How big of a threat is consolidation? Or do you think those companies will grow more by opening new formats? What about co-location and joint marketing opportunities?

12. How much do the food manufacturers play a role in the future of the store? How is category management affecting profits? Which manufacturers are more progressive and innovative? What kind of things are they doing? Are coupons still big? Does anyone ever redeem those things?

13. Where do you think you'll take the loyalty card program? What industries (hotel, airline?) are you taking lessons from, and applying to yours?

14. How is Wal-Mart's foray into grocery (Super Wal-Mart and Marketside) affecting your business? How about Tesco's Fresh and Easy?

15. Who do you think will be your competition in the future – not currently competing with you today?

Throughout this discussion, if Sharon mentioned a name of a company doing innovative, interesting things, I'd ask right then and there if she knew someone at that company. And then I'd say, "Great! I'd love to give them a call. Do you mind if I use your name?" If she gives me the okay, then I already have one contact to follow up with. I do this throughout the discussion. As I've said before, getting the names along with way removes all of the pressure of trying to secure contacts at the end.

Keep in mind, I haven't really spent any time in the grocery industry... unless you count the three weeks in college where I worked for Lawry's & Lipton – merchandising the shelves, refilling the taco seasoning tray (what's with our country's obsession with taco seasoning?), and dusting off the bottles of barbeque sauce. I quit after three weeks. It gave me headaches. It's giving me one right now just thinking about it.

I just came up with these questions because I've been to a grocery store. I've purchased food. I pass by the Starbucks on my way into the store. I pass by the bank and rental place on my way out. I shop at more than one chain (or at least run in to see what they're doing). I met some guy on a plane who sold cookies to store bakeries. (The trend there is inexpensive multi-packs – ten cookies for a dollar. They fly off the shelves!) I read an article about Tesco. And one about Wal-Mart. I'm no expert when it comes to the industry, but I do know how to get people talking. About this industry or any industry. It's all about asking smart questions.

Smart questions lead to interesting conversations, which lead to others opening up their networks to you. And the more people you talk to and learn from, the better your questions are, the more likely you'll be able to turn simple networking meetings into job offers (or really great relationships). Many of those same questions can apply to other industries by simply substituting a word or two.

Please do not ask the person, "How can I help you?" People who ask this question as a general statement have not done a good job of getting to know the other person. If you ask question after question and identify an opportunity to help someone, let them know. Otherwise, just be appreciative of the time that person gave you and call it a day.

Following Up

The first follow up action is to send a thank-you note. But, I'll ask the question: The thank-you note… important or insignificant? How many times do you hear how important it is to send a thank-you note after interviewing with a company? Should it be handwritten? Should it be sent over email?

I used to think it was important too. Years ago, I interviewed for a company to be its VP of Marketing. After my final interview, I sent off my carefully worded thank-you note along with a book (my favorite book of all time – *Competing For The Future,* by Gary Hamel and C.K. Prahalad) to my prospective boss, John. I got the job and was sure that my attention to detail certainly helped.

About a year into the job, I was in John's office in Philadelphia and saw the book. I'd forgotten that I'd sent it to him, and was so impressed that he, too, read my favorite book (bold, yet incorrect, assumption on my part!). I opened it up, only to find my thank-you note – seal intact – buried among the pages. He never read it. The book or the thank-you note! It was then that I realized it really didn't matter. No one cares if you send a thank-you note. If you're the wrong fit, it won't get you the job. If you're the right fit, it won't stop you from getting the job. It's nice. It's polite. It's the right thing to do. But critical? I don't think so.

That being said, I've learned a lot about thank-you notes. And if you're going to send one, you might want to consider this approach. Focus on sending a "you" letter. What's a "you" letter? Let me first show you what's NOT a "you" letter.

Not a You Letter

Dear Tom,

Thank you for meeting with me. I was really impressed with your organization. I can see how working with you would be very interesting. I enjoyed the team approach and I could easily see me fitting within the organization.

I look forward to hearing from you about next steps.
Molly

A You Letter

Dear Tom,

What an impressive organization you have! Your approach is fascinating and unlike most of the industry. It's amazing to see how the dynamic creates such incredible results.

Being an integral part of your expansion would be challenging and rewarding.

When can we discuss next steps?

Thank you,
Molly

The concept of a "you" letter is focusing your statements on the person to whom you're writing. It's all about them, and has nothing to do with you. It never starts sentences with the word "I." It's exciting and has enthusiasm with plenty of compliments and praise. And why not, who wants to receive a note full of negativity and criticisms?

The next time you meet with someone, do the polite thing and send them a thank-YOU note. It won't get you the job, but it might forge a stronger relationship.

And with that, I'd like to close this with a thank-you note to my sister, Mary.

Mary,

Thank you for hosting such a wonderful Thanksgiving Day. Eating at your house is always such a treat - mixed with just a little bit of adventure... pizza-oven roasted turkeys, sweet potato gnocchi in brown sugar and sage (the pilgrims had no idea what they were missing!), and 30+ people in an orderly line waiting to serve themselves after working up an appetite from the 23rd Annual Wendell Turkey Trot.

And it's just not Thanksgiving without your incredible selection of homemade desserts. Katy couldn't boast more about the cheesecake with chocolate frosting. And judging by the crumbs remaining... nor could anyone else.

Thank you for being my sister... and making the best pecan pie ever!

Love,
Molly

After the thank-you note, a good way to keep in contact (and therefore, on the person's mind) is to email a status of referrals, such as, "Thanks so much for referring me to John. We're meeting next week and I'm really looking forward to it!" If you're having trouble connecting with the referral, this is a good time to ask them to intervene and shoot off a quick email or voicemail requesting their contact meet with you.

This is also a good time to ask for other potential referrals, but only after you've proven that you're capable of following up on the ones they've given you in the first place. Don't forget… the more specific the request, the more terrific the response (e.g., John, do you happen to know anyone who works at Kelloggs or Hallmark?).

Networking Pitfall: Making Assumptions Why Someone Hasn't Responded

Let's say you contacted someone on Monday. It's now Wednesday and you're trying to figure out why that person is avoiding you! Here's a thought. It has nothing to do with you. That person is busy!

One of the worst things you can do is make assumptions for why someone hasn't responded to your influx of calls and emails.

I had a situation where someone contacted me to get a referral. He left a message. I was out of town. Three days later, he left another message. I was still out of town. Two days after that, he sent me an email saying, "I thought you were going to help me but I guess I was mistaken." Actually, I was going to help him, but I'm not now! If he gets uptight about me not calling back when I'm busy, what's he going to do to someone I refer him to? This was a year ago. And you know what? My life is no less fulfilled with him not being in it. But I can tell you that he missed out on a really great referral!

Another person I know, we'll call him Tad, was trying to get in touch with Greg. A couple weeks passed by and I asked Tad if he'd been able to connect with Greg. Tad replied, "Oh, he finally called me back." Sensing there was more to the story, I asked Tad what he did to get the magical response. He said he left Greg yet another message and said it was "improper not to respond."

Well, congratulations Tad, you won the battle and lost the war. Greg may have gotten back to you, but with that attitude, there's no way he's going to help you today, tomorrow or ever. He simply returned your call, checked the box off, and never has to talk to you again. However, your conversation just may have some really fascinating lingering effects. In fact, if there's ever an interaction between Greg and someone who brings up your name, I'm guessing Greg might suggest that you might be more than a tad annoying.

If you're so focused on people responding, then give them a good reason to respond. But don't forget, people can be busy. They can have great intentions (I usually do), but sometimes other priorities in life take precedence. Have some patience. Cut people some slack. And to pass the time, why don't you get busy contacting other people? If you're really networking with vengeance, you'll never even notice that someone hasn't responded!

Molly's Takeaway's

1. Referrals are always better than introductions because you have more control.
2. Meet with people in person rather than over the phone or email.
3. Avoid the common pitfalls. Be low maintenance. Communicate clearly. Be professional, but not too formal.
4. Follow up diligently on every lead but be patient, even if it seems like dog years have gone by.

Molly Wendell

CHAPTER 11: THE INTERVIEW

I honestly believe if you play your cards right, you'll get offers from your networking meetings. But, let's say you're doing things the old-fashioned way, and you're going through a formal process. And you've made it to the interview. That's great. Don't worry about being too available. Nobody wants to date that person who has nothing else going on! It's okay to be a little busy. It's okay to have to get back to them – after you've seen if you could change something in your schedule to make it work.

I've heard that you never want to go first. I'm not sure it matters. If you're the right person for the job, it won't matter what order you went in.

How to Secure a Call Back... and Possibly the Job!

In the interview, is it appropriate to ask for the job right then and there? Sometimes. Think about it from a sales perspective. A great salesperson will look for the right moment to ask for the order. Sometimes this is in the first meeting. Other times it's after a few meetings. Gauging when it's the right time to ask is crucial.

But really, it's more like the concept of dating. When you first meet someone, you're not necessarily trying to get married. You're simply trying to get to know each other to determine if this is someone with whom you want to spend more time. The object of the first date, then, is not to determine your future for the next umpteen years. It's to see if you can (and want to) secure another date (which really takes the pressure off both of you!). The only way to determine this is to ask questions. Listen to the responses and see if you're interested in taking it further. Give too much information, share your entire life story, and risk not being asked out again. Talk too much about your past relationships... and I guarantee you won't get a call back! Give just enough to whet the appetite, and say hello to a second date!

The same goes for you in the job search. When you first go to an interview, don't be so focused on trying to land the job. You should be more concerned with getting to the next round, or determining if you're even interested in getting to the next round. You need to learn more about the company, the hiring manager, the leadership. Are you on board with where they're going as a company? Do you fit with the company culture? Does it seem like an interesting place to work? Are the people fascinating? Will you be challenged?

Before you do that, however, why don't you start with a better understanding of the hiring process, so you know where you stand? Get this out of the way right away, so you're not rushing to ask at the end (or worse, forget to ask!). And be sure to take great notes the entire time! Take notes even if you think you'll remember. Taking notes makes it look like you're listening.

I remember interviewing with a company. I met with the hiring manager. My first question out of the gate was, "Tell me about the hiring process." He told me in the first round he was talking to about 25 people. "And how many people have you already spoken with?" I asked.

"Eight," he said. Then he was going to talk further to the top five candidates. Out of that, the top two would meet the president of the division. Good. My goal out of that meeting was not to land the job. It was to be one of the top five.

I wanted to get a handle on my competition. So I asked lots of questions relative to the type of person who would be a perfect fit. What are you looking for in a candidate? What do the other candidates have that I don't? What do I bring to the table that others don't? Which of those attributes (what others bring to the table or what I bring?) are more important? You never want to walk out of an interview and not know where you stand relative to your competition.

Satisfied that I understood the process, I started asking questions about the type of responsibilities this role would be given. What are the key initiatives that need to be tackled immediately? Beyond that, what would you like to see this person accomplish? In a perfect world, where would this person take this role? What responsibilities would you like to hand off so you can free yourself up for other things? And what would those other things be? Think about the preferred attributes... and try to tie them together with responsibilities. Based on this, are you moving up or down on the scale?

Do you think he's asked me a question yet? No, I haven't given him a chance. Do you think he cares? If he does, he's not showing it. He just keeps on talking.

By the end of our discussion, I knew that the role would be a fit. I was certainly well-qualified (by my assessment) and was pretty sure he thought so as well. Of course, how would he know? He never got a chance to ask me a question! Was I in the top five? I decided to find out. I dropped what's known in sales as a "trial balloon." I asked him, "When would you like me to meet the president?"

He said, "Let me set that up for next week." Here's what's great about that. I walked out of that first meeting knowing that I was one of the top two candidates. I also knew that for the right candidate, he was willing to bypass the process (and in case you're wondering, this is not uncommon).

A week later, I met with the president. The meeting with the president was similar. I asked all of the questions. He gave all of the answers. They offered me the job. I turned it down. I wasn't satisfied with their answers to my questions.

Another time I was meeting with a CEO for a VP of Marketing role. This CEO was obviously brilliant but just about the worst interviewer I'd ever met. He was distracted by everything. His answers were uninspiring. Even his tone of voice was blasé. I was so unimpressed with him that midway through the interview I told him, "You know, I'm interviewing you just as much as you're interviewing me. You might want to step it up." He did, and we had an interesting conversation. But, at the end of the day, is this someone I want to work for? Is this someone I'll learn something from? Is this someone who will inspire me? Probably not. I thanked him for his time. I didn't care if I heard from him again. There was no way I'd work in an organization with him at the helm.

You're probably wondering how I was able to turn these jobs down. I must have had another job lined up. Well, I didn't. It was more important to me to find the right fit, than just take something that I knew I wouldn't be extremely happy with. When you do that, those jobs don't last, and you'll just be looking again in a couple of months (and possibly miss out on the right fit because you were busy working in the wrong job). So don't do it to yourself, or to them!

So back to the question. Do you ask for the job at the interview? I'd say quit trying to get married, and focus more on trying to get that second date. Ask a question like, "Where do we take it from here?" And then let them respond (even if it takes them a while). If they still feel like they have to talk to a million more people, maybe you're not the one. In which case, it's better to move on. If they want to get back to you, be sure to ask when you can expect them to get back to you. Nail them down to a date and time. Make sure they see you write that date down. Ask them if they'd like you to follow up or will they? And then as you're leaving, thank them for their time and let them know you look forward to speaking with them on that date.

It's less threatening but still gives you an idea of where you stand. If you are a good fit, and you've had an interesting discussion, it should be pretty easy to secure that second date. If not, don't worry about it. Go find another company where the interest is mutual!

How Do You Dress?

This is easy. Dress professionally. Err on the side of dressing up versus dressing down. So what if you're the best dressed person in the room? I once met Larry. He told me that he no longer wears a suit and tie to an interview. In fact, he keeps his tie in the car and watches people go in and out of the building to see how they're dressed. If the men are wearing a tie, he wears one. If not, he doesn't. He claimed that he lost out on an opportunity because he was too dressed up. Maybe he lost out because someone saw him lurking in the parking lot and thought his stalk-ish ways were just a little bit creepy.

Another person, Jim, told me he landed a job because he was dressed casually. He was on his second interview, they called him in and he didn't have time to change. Since when do you not have time to change? It's an interview, not a 911 call. Plan ahead. Either way, he showed up in jeans, and claimed they hired him because "he looked like them."

I would submit that in both of these cases, the person was hired or wasn't hired because of how they were dressed. They were hired/not hired because they were the right/not the right person for the job. If you're the right candidate, and they know it, the presence or absence of a tie is not going to be the deciding factor. And if it is, wow. What an easy interview process!

Prepping for the Interview

Before you go into an interview, be sure to do your research. Research the company. Check the website. Read the press releases. Understand their products and services. Take a look at their customers. Research their competitors. Have a clue.

After you've done the company research, find out about the people you're interviewing with. Check their bio. Google them. See if you know anyone who knows them. Call them up and get the scoop. Check with previous employers. Maybe they're already doing this on you.

My friend, Lisa, called me one day. She told me she was interviewing a person she thought I might have worked with, and could I give her some insight? Absolutely, what do you want to know?

It's the best kind of a reference check a company can do – an unsolicited one. A reference check outside the policy handbook of Human Resources. And don't think for a minute this doesn't happen all the time. What are your previous coworkers saying about you? Maybe you should make sure those bridges are still intact.

Interview Pitfall: Lack of Preparedness

Nothing's worse than heading into a meeting without doing some sort of prep work. I once had a meeting with a guy named David. I walked into his office and saw a rather sizable aquarium (that looked like it was directed by Tim Burton – and could've used a little cleaning, by the way). Fortunately, I had done my research and learned that David was a huge fan of fish and the aquarium concept. He belongs to some aquarium groups and regularly contributes to their discussion boards.

If I hadn't known this, I probably would've walked in, seen the aquarium and started into a diatribe of how I think aquariums and pet fish are the biggest waste of time and money ever. I mean what's interesting about staring at a fish in a murky container? Oh look, its gills opened. Oh, now it went under that rock. Want to watch me feed it? No, I don't as a matter of fact. What I'd prefer is to watch you not feed it. Try that for many days in a row, and then see what happens. Maybe then you'll clean that thing. It's disgusting and it smells!

That meeting could've been a catastrophe, but I did my research. I held back, and didn't dare go there… because that would do nothing to ingratiate myself to David.

If you have a meeting with someone, hopefully you've done some research to uncover a little bit more about the person, identify some common bonds, and avert potential disasters. At least do the basic things such as Googling them, reading a bio, finding out what community or charity events they partake in. There's really a fine line between being prepared and stalking, right?!

When you meet with the person, armed with so much knowledge about them, there's no need to divulge it all. Little things can be dropped into the conversation very casually. I remember sitting in a job interview a few years back, and was meeting with a woman named Dana. Prior to our meeting, I read her bio and saw that she was involved in a charity called Logopedics. Never heard of it? I'm not surprised. In fact, no one has heard of it. Other than those women who were in the sorority of Kappa Alpha Theta in college. Immediately, I thought, she must be a Theta. I checked the Alumna directory and sure enough, there was her name. We shared that in common.

The first thing I said when we met was, "Guess where I was this weekend?" Given that we'd never even met before, she had no idea. I said, "I went to Grand Convention! Can you believe it?" I didn't even mention the word Theta because I knew she'd know.

She replied, "No... no I can't believe it!" I think what she couldn't believe was the fact that I knew she was a Theta Alum. I told her a little about the convention, and how impressed I was with the women I'd met. Then, I asked her about her involvement in the local alum chapter. We had a great conversation – which actually turned into a job offer.

I didn't need to tell her how I knew. I didn't need to go into detail about the research. I just put it out there, talked about it for a minute and then moved on.

What I like better than finding activities is finding people we both know. Checking LinkedIn to find out who they know – that you know – is probably the easiest way. But there are plenty of other ways. Are they a coach on a Little League baseball team? Look at the team roster and figure out if you know any parents. Are they on the board of a charity? See if you know anyone else on the board. Where did they work before? Do you know anyone at the old company? Where do they live? Maybe you know some of their neighbors? What about college? Maybe you know some of their classmates?

You'll be amazed what you find if you just do a little research. And you'll be even more amazed at how you're able to turn a good meeting into a great one simply because you took the time to find out a little about that person (and how much they love pet fish)!

What Do You Bring?

I'm amazed at the number of people who show up at an interview empty-handed. That's it. No paper, no pen, no resume, no nothing. All I can think is... who's going to take notes for you? How are you going to remember anything? Is that how you're going to show up for an important meeting once you're on the job? Empty-handed? Unprepared?

Now don't go overboard either... and bring too much (like it's your first day on the job!).

Here's what you want to bring with you to every interview:

1. Portfolio or some kind of folder to hold your resume.

2. Notepad. Make sure it's not a brand new notepad. Have at least a few pages written on. Preferably from another interview. Make it look like you're busy. Make it look like you're talking to other people and aren't just going to take the first thing that comes along. Make it look like you're important. Because you are! Your time is valuable. And you're going to do your own due diligence to ensure this is the right fit for you.

3. Resume. Never start off the interview by trying to hand them your resume. Wait until they ask for it. Hopefully, they never will. The best interviews are the ones where nobody's looking at your resume. When I was interviewing, the moment I would see someone start to peruse my resume, I knew the meeting was headed nowhere fast. At that point, I'd quickly ask a question. I'm not ashamed of my resume. Actually, I'm pretty proud of it. I've done a lot of great things. But I know our time is limited, and I don't want to waste any of it with one person reading in silence.

4. A pen. In fact, bring two pens in case the first one doesn't work. Having to borrow a pen shows how unprepared you are. Who doesn't have a pen that works? Why would I want this pen-less person working for me? Is she going to steal pens from the office supply

cabinet for personal use? I don't know, but I'm not going to wait around to find out.

What Do You Say?

Don't wait for them to control the interview. That's your job. Show them you're the person who won't just sit around and wait for other people to tell you what to do. Show them you're the person who will take control and ownership of the situation. They will be able to count on you to get the job done.

The interview is a two-way street. People forget that too often. They expect the interviewer to be prepared. To have all the questions ready. To control the flow of the meeting. I say forget that! You're interviewing them just as much as they're interviewing you. You might as well figure out whether you're even interested in working for this company.

I once interviewed with a company. My first round was with the Senior VP of Marketing. He invited me back to meet with the members of his team. I spent five hours that day, one hour with each person. I have to say I wasn't overly impressed with what would be my peers. In fact, I kind of thought that most, if not all, should be replaced. When I went back in to meet with the Sr. VP, based on the team's feedback, he told me that I probably wasn't a good fit for the team. His team seemed to like me, but the majority of them thought I was too competitive.

This didn't surprise me at all, I said. In fact, I am competitive. That's oftentimes what makes me a great employee. It was apparent that it wasn't a good fit. His biggest challenge to being successful was not going to be the product or the competitors. It was going to be that he had a bunch of casual players on his team. And if he didn't replace them, he wouldn't compete effectively. Because this wasn't the team that was going to win the Olympics. This was the team that was going to show up at the Opening Ceremony – not as athletes, not as the organizers, but as spectators. He lasted another few months, but ultimately left the company because he was surrounded by a bunch of nice people who had no drive to succeed.

Getting turned down could be the best thing that ever happens to you. At the time, it doesn't always feel that way. But really, sometimes you just don't fit. Sometimes you don't know until you have that first, second, or third interview. But when you really don't fit, you know it. And at this company, I really didn't fit. I was disappointed because on the surface, it sounded like a great opportunity. But as I got deeper into it, I realized I wouldn't have been happy there. It's better to know that and move on, than waste your time on an opportunity that really is anything but.

How Do You Control the Interview?

That's easy. Just ask all of the questions. Control the flow. Ask for further clarification if you want. When you don't, move on. When you're ready to end it… close the sale.

But what kind of questions do you ask? My very good friend, Scott, once shared his secret of interviewing. The first thing he asks – right off the bat – is, "What's your ideal candidate? What kind of skill set are you looking for? Traits? Attributes?" As the hiring manager describes the ideal candidate, Scott is taking copious notes. He then spends the rest of the interview feeding them back with all of the things they said were important in a candidate.

But how do you control it when they're asking the questions? That's easy. Just start off by saying, "Before we get started, can I ask you a question?" If they've already asked you a question, just say, "Before I answer that, can I ask you a question?" Of course they'll say yes. From there, you never stop asking questions. Just keep them coming. Don't give them an opportunity to ask you a question.

I once had a phone interview with a CEO. I used that same line. "Jim, before we get started, can I ask you a question?" After about an hour, he said, "Can I ask you a question now?"

I jokingly said, "Actually, I'm out of time." Really, he asked? I told him I was kidding – and what did he want to know. He asked two questions – of no particular consequence, and we finished our call. I was offered the job. Jim didn't care that he didn't get to ask questions in the interview. He was more impressed with the type of questions I was asking.

But what if they have all of these questions they're supposed to get answered? Who cares? Don't you have all of these questions that you need to get answered? Isn't this about finding the right place for you? Do you dare walk out of there without understanding where the company is headed? Which ship are you going to work for? The Apollo or the Titanic? Don't you want to find out before you get on board?

What questions are going to get you the offer letter? Smart questions. Questions about the business, the industry, the competition, the products, the services, new markets. You name it.

What questions are going to get you the rejection letter? Stupid questions. Questions about health-care benefits, holidays, 401K plans, working hours (unless it's a shift-type position).

With an unprepared interviewer, controlling the interview is easy. With a more structured interviewer, it takes a little more finesse. When I run across this person, I let them have a few questions, I take a few, and then let them have a few more. But I only answer the questions I want to.

Stupid Questions. Smart Answers.

Sometimes your interviewer is not very good, and has come up with a list of stupid questions – some of which you may end up having to answer. Here are some approaches to the tired, old, uninteresting interview questions.

What's your greatest weakness? One of my most favorite questions is the age old, "What are your weaknesses?" We all have them. After all, we're only human. I take this question as an opportunity to talk about all of the things I absolutely hate doing – and would loathe in a job. Therefore, if that's what the job consists of, I'm better off not getting it! For example, I always say, "I'm not the person who's interested in routine/maintenance type work. If that's the majority of the job, then I'm not your person. If you've already outlined the strategy and are simply looking for someone to implement, I'm not the right fit. On the other hand, if you're looking for someone to develop the strategy, and figure out how to be more competitive (there I go again… with the competitiveness!), then I'm the person. If you're looking for a change agent who isn't satisfied with the way it's always been done, but is looking for new ways to improve the business and take it to the next level, I'm the person."

Notice how I didn't mention the word weakness? Notice how I really didn't bring up a weakness? Notice how I simply identified aspects of a job that don't interest me whatsoever, turned it around to what does interest me, and wrapped it all up in a nice package and handed it back to them with a pretty bow as to where I'd really fit. That's what you do with that question! Next!

I was talking to a friend, Elizabeth, an engineer. She was telling me how she hates when people ask that question. I told her it was such a great opportunity to put something out on the table they may be thinking of but not want to say. I said, "You're kind of intense. Maybe that's what you could say." And she was so excited.

She was intense. And it could be perceived as negative or positive – depending on the person doing the perceiving.

The next interview she went on was a group interview. That question was asked, and she said, "I'm kind of intense. And sometimes it can be perceived as a little too intense, and turn some people off." A couple of people in the room related to that statement and they started talking about it.

"Yes, me too. I get that from people all of the time."

"Yes, me too. I hate it when people accuse me of that, but that's who I am."

Turns out, Elizabeth found herself among peers, and they really related to her. She got the offer… and now they can all be intense together.

What do you see yourself doing in five years? Well, I certainly don't see myself sitting in the same office, that's for sure. And I'm probably not working with you anymore because you were fired for asking stupid questions like that. Where does anyone see themselves in five years? I'm not sure. Maybe you're like my friend, Ruth, and have a five, ten, and twenty-year plan. Or maybe you're like the rest of us and don't know where you see yourself in six months. This is not the time to talk about how you've always wanted to become a Horse Whisperer or take three months to trek through Nepal. No, this is the time to be vague. Very vague.

Here's how I'd answer that question, "Well, that's an interesting question. I'd see myself with much more responsibility, more scope, perhaps launching new products into more geographic markets. Maybe an international assignment? It's tough to say being outside the company looking in, but I would imagine it would have lots to do with expanding the business." Then I'd turn it around to them. "What about you. Where do you expect to be in the next five years... or even three?" I'm amazed how many people I've met with have told me of their desire to be elsewhere... in another company or another business altogether. It's astounding!

What are you looking for in a job? One that pays on a regular basis? What else? This is a lousy in-person question. Isn't this the type of information you want to know prior to them showing up? Perhaps it could've been used to screen some people out. Since they didn't, looks like you're going to have to answer it. Now, don't you wish you were controlling the interview with your own questions?

The reality is that many people can do the job, but finding the right candidate almost always comes down to the right fit. Therefore, I answer this with, "Well, all things being equal, I'm more focused on the fit within the company. The team. Ensuring that I like the people I'll be working with. I want to be surrounded by a team of A players – who are smart and work hard. I want to be proud to call them my colleagues. And I want them to be proud to call me theirs as well." How's that for sucking up?

What would others say about you? They'd say I'm the greatest person alive. Isn't that what you want to hear? So, yes, greatest person alive. Final answer.

What motivates you? Again... stupid question to ask during the meeting. Should have had it in a pre-screen. If you're in sales, you need to ensure your answer has money in there at some point – but it can't be the only thing. For everyone else, don't you dare say money. What motivates me? A challenge. An obstacle. Someone saying something can't be done. Walking on water. Healing the blind. Performing miracles.

Why are you the best person for the job? Are you kidding me? Why are you the worst interviewer ever? This is exactly how I'd answer this one, "Interesting question. Let me ask you something.

141

Based on what you know about me and what you know about the other candidates, how do you think I compare? What makes me more interesting? What do others have that I don't have?" Get them to tell you why you're the best person for the job.

Tell me about yourself. I can tell you about myself in one word. Google. Don't you do your homework before you embark on an interview? Guess not. The best way to answer this is: What do you want to know? An even better way to answer this is: Well, I could go on, but real quick, let me ask you a question. And take control of this interview before they ruin your chances of having a good conversation!

Why do you want to work here? Oh, I don't know. Because you seem like you're hiring? Bad answer. Why do I want to work here? You obviously want to say something about the "excellent opportunity for advancement"… blah blah blah. But what I would do is say something like, "I've done a lot of research about the industry, the players and this company. You're right where I want to be. I like where the company is headed. I've been really impressed by the people I've met. I see opportunity to really make an impact. And it really feels like it could be a great fit for both of us!"

How Knowing Nothing Will Get You More Job Offers Than Knowing Everything

I was in yoga class, and right behind me was a new student — we'll call him Chuck. He set up his mat in the hottest part of the room. One of the teachers told him that he might want to move because it gets really hot, and given it was his first time, it might be better to move. But "No," Chuck said, "I want to get a good workout."

Within ten minutes, Chuck was curled up in child's pose — gasping for air. Chuck's version of down dog looked more like dead dog. Halfway through the class, Chuck lay prostrate as though he himself was on his last leg. But Chuck figured he'd come into the class... and be a superstar. He tried to cram all of his yogic experience into one class. I don't know if Chuck will be back.

What might have served Chuck better was to seek first to understand. Understand the process. Understand the poses. Understand that the heat won't kill you, but it just might set you back a few if you didn't drink enough water (or had one too many drinks of something else the night before).

And this got me thinking about interviews. So often, people tell me, "I'm going to go in there and show them. I'm going to tell them everything I can do for them. I'm going to get them to see that I'm the perfect person because I have all the answers. I'm going to... blah, blah, blah...."

Here's the reality. You know nothing. Are you planning to go in and insult everyone who has been working there (a lot longer than you have!) by telling them you know more about their company than they do? Just because they're bringing in someone from the outside to get fresh insights and, shake things up, doesn't mean they don't know anything.

How about the next time you're brought in for an interview, forget about you and all that you don't know, and focus on them, and all that they do know. Ask them what you want to know. Where is the company going? What is the company doing to get ahead of the competition? Which competitor are they most worried about today? What about five years from now? What new markets are they getting into? How do they plan to make that happen? What percent share do they have of their customer's dollar? How are they planning to get more? How is the team positioned? Where are the holes? What makes this a great place to work? What's the attrition rate? When good people leave, where do they go? What attracted them to the job? What's one thing they wish they had known prior to working there? What surprised them most once they got on board? If they were to do one thing differently, what would it be?

Are you supposed to be a change agent? Then you'd better ask some questions about change. Ask about decision making and how quickly or slowly it occurs. What about cultural issues – and people's difficulty with change? What percent of the employees are change agents? Or will you be the only one (I hope you're getting paid a lot!). Who's going to get in the way... and why? What happened to the last change agent (may s/he rest in peace)?

Quit focusing on what you can do for them, and start asking the smart questions that will help you get a clearer picture of the real opportunity. The more you discover, the more you might find you have no desire to work at this company or for this person. Or, you might find that the opportunity sounds even more exciting than ever! Either way, you won't know this unless you do a little interrogation. Take a lesson from Chuck. Seek first to understand. Ask the right questions. Pace yourself. And save enough to come back the next day.

What if you've done such a great job of controlling the interview that they didn't get a chance to answer everything on their list? That's a good sign. If it's really important to them, you can say, "Uh oh, we didn't get to all of your questions. Is there anything you absolutely need to ask? Let's get that covered so you can check it off the list."

How Can You Tell When a Company Is Just Not That Into You?

I was in the Dallas airport and ran into a guy that I dated a while back. Well, to say we dated is probably an extreme. We went on two dates. I thought they were pretty good. The first was at least good enough to get him to ask me out again. But after the second one, he didn't call back. Maybe he just got really busy at work?

Maybe he was in a terrible accident and was in a coma for a while? Or maybe he just wasn't that into me.

This reminds me a lot of the job search. How many times have you had a great meeting with an HR or hiring manager – only to never hear back from them again? Maybe they lost your number? Maybe they got a huge project dumped on them by the CEO – and are pulling all-nighters to get it done? Or maybe, just maybe, they're just not that into you.

Finding the right fit at a company is a lot like a relationship. And when it's right, and I mean really right, it usually happens pretty quickly.

What are the signs they're just not that into you?

They extend the hiring process longer than expected. This typically happens when they haven't quite found the right fit. And they don't want to settle. And neither do you. Settling is almost always a short-term situation that gets fixed pretty quickly. Is this the job you really wanted? Is this the company you really wanted? Maybe there were a few things about the job, the company (or even the people) that weren't perfect, but you were willing to tolerate.

I remember interviewing with a company where the VP of Sales told me he had a pretty innovative sales recognition strategy. He'd get on the intercom system and say, "Great job, Dave!" That was it. That was his big strategy for motivating the sales force to perform at higher-than-ever levels. What's next, a limbo contest? Yep, right after the hotdog eating contest (always a big morale booster!). Then to show the employees they really cared, the entire executive team was going to serve lunch to all employees in the cafeteria. I could've worked at that company. I could've worn the chef's hat while dishing out the pork 'n beans. Most probably, I would've been settling. Most definitely, I would've gone home every night wondering why I chose to work with a bunch of schmucks.

145

Forget about settling. Go figure out where you really want to work, and target those companies. Who cares if they don't have a posting? Most never will – and they still manage to make hiring decisions. Amazing, isn't it?!

Your contact within the company has stopped returning your calls. No matter how many times you call. And fortunately they don't realize it's you because you don't leave a message. Hey stalker, catch a clue. Many, many, many companies have caller ID. They know it's you. They're not picking up on purpose. Put the phone down, get out of the house, and go meet some other companies that can use a speed dialer like you!

You're one of the final two candidates and the executive team has to regroup to make a decision. But they're busy, and schedules aren't working out so it's taking a while. Chances are, they offered the other candidate the position and are waiting to see if that person takes it. Congratulations! You were one of the top candidates. Think about how many people didn't even make it as far in the process as you! Take your second place trophy, toss it in the garage with your grade school memories, and move on. Go find the company where you will be number one! It's out there and it's waiting for you. So hurry up.

When a company is not that into you, it's okay. Here's the thing. Not hearing back is actually a good thing. It means you're not the right fit. It frees you up to go find a company where you will be the right fit. One-way relationships aren't fun for anyone. So quit prolonging the pain. Get out there. Meet more people. Build more relationships. And "save the pretty" for someone who deserves it!

And what happened with that guy? It doesn't really matter. Turns out, I just wasn't that into him either.

Landing a Job Is Just Like Sales 101 – Get to Know Your Customer

When I was in training at IBM (back when companies used to actually train you!), one of my classes was on sales calls. The instructor gave us the outline of what we'd be graded on. We needed to go through the five phases of the selling process. If I recall correctly, it was something like: Develop Rapport, Uncover Needs, Propose a Solution, Demo the Product, Close the Sale.

Just before my first graded call, I was walking up the stairs with a cup of coffee and a muffin. I tripped on a step, spilled the coffee all over my dress, dropped my muffin… not a good way to start the day. But I went into the meeting with a smile on my face, determined to make the most of it (despite the fact that I stunk like a two-day-old cup o' Joe).

When I was given my results, I fared pretty poorly. Just about all I did right was show up. Actually, come to think of it, I was graded down because I walked in five minutes late (due to my unfortunate coffee spill). Maybe all I did right was leave?

But every call was like that for me. If it wasn't scoring poorly on one aspect, it was another. It seems like I couldn't do anything right.

When that five-week stint ended, the class rankings were sent off to our branch office. I came in forty-eighth out of fifty. My only saving grace was that the other person from the Los Angeles branch came in forty-ninth. All I thought was, "Who could possibly do worse than us? That person must have spilled the coffee on the customer!" I vowed to do better, but in reality, I didn't understand what I did wrong, why I always got a lousy score. Maybe they just didn't like me?

After a successful career at IBM, always hitting my numbers, always making the 100% Club, I didn't worry too much about the class scores. But a few years later, I finally realized what I did wrong. I was so focused on checking off the steps of the process that I forgot to just sit down and have a conversation.

And that's exactly what people in the job search do. They're so focused on answering questions about their strengths and weaknesses (or the fact that they don't really "see anything they do as a weakness"... uh, sure) that they forget the person across the table is just that... a person. Someone who would be far more impressed if you knew how to have an interesting, engaging conversation.

Landing a job is Sales 101 – only you're selling yourself (legally). Everyone knows that people buy from people they like. If you can get the person across the table to like you, your chances of them buying are greater. And how do you get someone to like you? Get them to talk about themselves. It's that easy.

Quit being so focused on the process. Be focused on the person. Be genuinely interested in them, their company, their challenges, their opportunities. Ask the smart, provocative questions that get them talking about these things. Ask questions that get them thinking. Ask questions that get them realizing that you probably know what you're talking about – or could at least figure it out. And pretty soon, you will be the person on the other side of the table!

Just go easy on the people who spill on themselves. The outside may have a stain or two, but it's what's on the inside that really matters!

How Do I Stay in Touch Without Being a Pest?

Anne went through a round of interviews and thought it went really well. She followed up with a thank-you note and hadn't heard from the company in two weeks. She knew they were in a rush to hire someone and really wanted it to be her. She asked me what to do. Here's what I told her.

First, exercise patience. When you're in the job search, your definition of "a rush" and a company's definition are two different things. Unfortunately, when you're tasked with hiring someone, you don't get to shirk all other corporate duties to focus completely on the hiring process. It really just adds more work to your already overloaded plate. A rush to them might be forty-five days (let's hope they're not working for 911!).

Second, and this is something you need to do when you're in the interview, ask what the interview process is, the time lines and when they plan to make a decision. Ask them how firm they will be on those dates. Then, add two to four weeks to those dates (at least) to properly set your expectation.

Third, if you really feel compelled to follow up again, don't just send a "checking in" email or a "haven't heard from you and got really worried that you completely forgot about me and how great I am and the perfect person for the position" phone call. Do this: Find an interesting, timely, relevant article about something you discussed in the interview. Again, make it relevant – and hopefully something they may not have seen. A few years back, I was waiting to hear from a company about a position. After the final rounds of interviews (where I was the only candidate left), I called HR a few times and never heard back. I sent an email to the president along with an interesting article from *Fortune* magazine – essentially showcasing some of the challenges and opportunities we had discussed in the interview. About sixty seconds after I hit send, the president emailed me back and asked to schedule a call with me.

This time when I called my HR contact and left yet another voicemail; letting him know I heard from the president requesting a call, and did he happen to know the details, I heard back from them immediately. (It's almost like they were screening the call. Do people actually do that?!)

Be patient. Know the process. Be relevant. Or better yet, close the deal if you can while you're still meeting with them face-to-face.

Molly's Takeaways

1. Do your homework. Get all the background information you need to help you really know what's going on with the company and the decision makers.
2. Show up prepared to hold up your end of the interview process. Have your questions ready.
3. Have a smart answer ready for any stupid questions. Then don't let them ask any more questions. The interview isn't about you. Focus on them, their needs, expectations, plans for the future.
4. Learn their time line to fill the position and then follow up in a relevant way.

CHAPTER 12: BEING RELEVANT

I remember applying for a scholarship in college. It was for the San Diego Grocers Association. The criteria spelled out that you had to be a marketing student in good standing. I had just gotten a job with Lawry's & Lipton. I thought that would be perfect. I'm a marketing student working in the grocery industry. Of course I could compete effectively for the scholarship. I filled out the paperwork, waxed eloquent on the impact of the grocery industry – and the changes it was going through. I integrated my daily work experiences into my essay – giving a first-hand glance at the challenges and opportunities the industry faced.

Nine months later, I received a call saying I was a finalist for the scholarship. After the in-person interviews, I was notified that I won. Of course I was going to win. I was the perfect candidate! I don't know how many other marketing students were in the grocery industry, but I can tell you that the Grocer's Association wasn't about to award the scholarship to anyone in any other industry!

With Skills Like Yours, Why Would Anyone Want to Hire You?

I was having a conversation the other day with someone from IBM. They just announced some layoffs, and it was going to affect a few thousand people… this time. As we contemplated the people who would be left without a desk, we got to talking about how so many people leave a company, and are basically unprepared to work for another company. I mean, they know nothing that's of any relevance to anyone else.

Perhaps you got soft working at the same company for twenty years. Perhaps you didn't keep up with new technologies. Perhaps you let your skills slide a little bit. Perhaps you didn't interact with people from other businesses. Perhaps all you did was work.

151

Whatever the reason, I have to ask you – why do you think you're going to be relevant to anyone else?

Take Nancy. Nancy was having an interview with a weight management company. And she was really excited about it. I asked her how she was preparing for the interview. She said she studied up on the company. What about the competitors? What about the suppliers? What about potential new markets? What about key influencers? I tell you what, if I was going to interview with a weight management company, you know what I'd do? I'd go meet with everybody and anybody in that industry. Competitors. Doctors. Nutritionists. Schools. Associations (American Heart Association, American Diabetes Association). Overeaters Anonymous. McDonalds (to see what they're doing to help cure obesity in this country – because the whole trans fat thing is simply not enough). Gastric Bypass Clinics. Fitness Centers. Pharmaceutical Firms. Health Food Stores. Online weight tracking systems. The people who invented the BodyBug. Nike. Anybody and everybody who focuses on weight. Heck, I'd probably call Oprah.

What would I learn? I don't know yet. That's why I'm talking to them. But, I bet I'll walk away from the conversation knowing more than I did before I got there. I want to find out what's going on. Who's doing what? Any interesting trends (other than we're getting fatter)? Any breakthroughs? What I want to do is gather enough data, so when I'm in that interview with the weight management company, it's obvious I know the industry. I'm asking all the right questions. I'm up on the trends. I'm up on the issues. I'm familiar with the players. I know people. I'm relevant.

It reminds me of a time when I did a presentation for a commercial insurance brokerage. I didn't know much about the inner workings of the business. But, I figured other people who'd been in that industry did. I called competitors (thanks LinkedIn!) and asked people for a few minutes of their time. They gave me more than a few. I called customers and asked how they made insurance decisions. I called suppliers and found out how they perceived this company – relative to others they did business with. I spoke to previous employees to find out their experiences. And I repeated this in a few markets, so I'd have a good handle on any regional differences. I did my research.

By the time I went in for my presentation, I knew as much about their business as an outsider could. I knew what they did well. I knew what they did poorly. I knew their reputation. I knew why they won deals... and lost them. I knew why people left. I used specific examples – only an insider would understand. And my presentation was well received. Because it was relevant. I was relevant.

I know a lot of people who are looking to get into the Alternative Energy industry. What they're doing is applying for positions and trying to meet people in these firms so they can get an interview. What about taking a class? What about attending a conference? What about reading books and magazines on the subject? What about talking to people already in the industry? And I don't necessarily mean people working at the company you want to work for. I mean everybody else. I mean every solar panel manufacturer.

Why don't you call the solar panel installer and have them come to your house and quote you on installing solar panels (let's hope you don't live on the fifth floor of a ten-story hi-rise!). What about the local university? Who's involved in alternative energy there? Talk to some scientists. Talk to some analysts. Talk to someone who works for the utility company. Talk to someone who works for the city, the state, the country. Talk to a reporter who just did an article about the industry. Talk to everybody! And really find out what's going on. And really know what's going on. And then, you'll be relevant. Then, when you are finally talking to someone at a company you really want to work for, you've already done your research. You're already knowledgeable. And perhaps, you'll find that you're extremely relevant.

Be Relevant With Your Skills

I remember when I was looking for a VP of Marketing role. I often think back during that time and ask myself what I could've done differently. And I know exactly what I could've done. I could've gotten more relevant. I was good at my job, but I wasn't on the cutting edge.

If I were to do it all over again, I would've taken that extra time on my hands (that two years of extra time!) and gotten really smart on the up and coming technologies in marketing. At that time it was search engine optimization. If I had taken that time to build my skills and become a VP of Marketing with an SEO specialty, I know I would've landed a great position. I know there would've been opportunities even in a down market. But, I didn't think about that until it was two years too late (and I was already down the path toward a new career in a new industry).

Think about your functional area and what's on the cutting edge. And learn that skill. And become more relevant than any of your competition.

Maybe you're like my college friend, Carl. Carl liked to refer to himself as "Mr. Do the Minimal." He was a solid C-player. Guess what? In a market like today's, C-players don't get hired. You need to bring your A-game. You need to have real skills. And you need to have real relevance.

Maybe you were one of the thousands of people who got laid off. Why don't you take all of this extra time on your hands and get relevant? Get relevant by industry. Get relevant by technology. Get relevant by functional area. Whatever you do, get relevant! And you just might find that what you've done for the past five to ten years is less relevant than what you're about to do for the next five to ten weeks!

Be Relevant to the Needs of the Business

One of the most exciting days of the year happens in mid-April. Yep, that's right. Draft Day for the National Football League. Because to me, that only means one thing. Football season (my favorite time of the year) is just around the corner! Few stages exist where landing a job is such a public act. I can't think of too many others, except for maybe our presidential election, oh, and American Idol.

Much goes into selecting the right person for the team. Coaches (and sometimes management) evaluate the team, find the holes (the same ones the opponents found in the previous season!), and look for individuals who would be both a fit for the position as well as a fit within the organization. Rarely is it a highly strategic decision (although I'm certain some would disagree with me). And oftentimes, all of the work going into the selection might be hastily disregarded because a player they didn't think would be available still is (e.g., the Arizona Cardinals and Matt Leinart in 2006).

When you think about it, it's not unlike other companies. A company will evaluate its current need and make a tactical decision to hire someone. It is very rare anymore to find a company that makes strategic hires the majority of the time (meaning… "we want you on the team and we'll figure out where later"). And, over the lifespan of a company, needs change. One day, they might be looking for someone to expand the business rapidly. The next, they're looking for a turnaround expert (because the predecessor expanded too quickly?). Either way, what you need to think about in your job search is, what do I bring to the table? Where do I fit in? And then align that with the companies that require your kind of expertise.

Just because you're a great business developer doesn't mean the company needs your skills. Recently, Andrew came to one of our Executives Network meetings. He knows how to sell. His problem is that his company doesn't know how to deliver. Right

155

now, they don't need Andrew. They need an operations specialist who can get the business to deliver on what Andrew sold. The most important thing for Andrew – as he looks for his next position – is to evaluate the company's operations and ensure they are equipped to deliver. Otherwise, he'll end up where he is today... looking for a job.

In an economy like this, companies are looking for tactical hires. Filling a role for where they are in the life cycle of the company. Sometimes they're expanding. Sometimes they're contracting. Sometimes they're on a marketing roll. Sometimes they're on a layoff roll.

As you evaluate which companies you want to work for, take a close look at which stage the company is in. Determine not only if this is the right company for you, but is the company in the right stage of its life cycle for you? Sometimes a company that wasn't a fit a few years back is a perfect fit now. And sometimes a company that isn't a fit today just might be ready for you in a couple of years. Doing your homework here could make the difference between a lot of companies interested in you... and none interested in you.

Be Relevant to Others

They absolutely amaze me. Those people who come to a job search meeting with the sole mission of getting help. They sit with their arms crossed, completely tuned out and wait for their turn. When it finally comes, they give their background and ask the group for help with some contacts. Once their turn is over, they go back to tuning everyone else out.

How do I know this? It's easy to spot who is paying attention. They're the ones that get involved and give constructive input. The ones who are not paying attention are easy to spot too! They're the ones that tell the group they spent twenty years at Boeing. This helpful piece of information is mentioned only after three other people in the room have already requested contacts at Boeing and no one said boo. Maybe they didn't want to give their contacts to those people? Really? You can't tell me that after twenty years at Boeing you don't have a contact list of at least 20 people (more likely 200). And you can't find one to give to someone who needs help? Maybe, you're thinking, I don't want to give my contacts out to those people, because I don't really know them. Maybe others are thinking the same about you!

If you're not helpful to others, why should anyone be helpful to you? If you leave the meeting and didn't feel like you got a lot out of it, you might want to ask yourself, how much did you give? How many contacts did you offer up? How many people did you help? How many connections did you make for others? Don't just sit in the room and take up space. Be an active participant. Pay attention and get the most out of the meeting you possibly can. Be positive and proactive. Be the person others want to refer.

When Executives Network first started, it was a small group (with a different name). We had about 40 total participants – with 15 to 20 showing up at each meeting. We'd take turns facilitating the meeting. On this particular day, Malcolm was running the meeting. Ten people went ahead of me, and I took copious notes about each one. My thought was that if I didn't have a contact for them today, perhaps I would meet someone over the course of the next few weeks and be able to create a connection.

But, I always tried to think of a contact for each one of them right then. Someone relevant. If it wasn't someone from their target company, it was someone I knew from their industry. Or maybe their functional area. Or maybe someone I just thought they'd like to know personally. After all, I'd been networking like crazy and I'd built up a nice database of contacts.

Just as I was about to take my turn, Malcolm stopped me. He said, "Before we go on, I'd like to say something. I don't know if everyone's noticed, but there's one person in the room that has helped every single person so far. And she does this every meeting. And for this, I would like to award this gold medal. The number one connector." And he came over and put the medal around my neck. It was so cool. I felt like a million bucks. (Trust me, after getting rejected in the job search for so long, it's the little wins each day that keep you going!) I also felt incredible pressure to deliver a contact for every person who went after me!

I still have that medal. And it's a great reminder to always be on the lookout for others. Helping them made me feel good. But as it turns out, there was great benefit in it for me. The more people I helped, the more people helped me. And they were happy to. Just like I was happy to help them.

The next time you're at a job search meeting, or any networking event really, think about how you might be able to help each person that you meet. That's what makes you someone others want to know. And it gets you in doors you never thought possible.

When People Want to Help You, Let Them

But be worthy of their help. Oftentimes at our Executives Network meetings, people will end their request for help by telling everyone what companies they can help with. One person in particular comes to mind. Kevin would always end his turn with, "And I can help you with the following companies…." What a waste of our time. Did someone previously ask for help at those companies? Then speak up when they ask. Maybe you weren't listening. Quit zoning out and start paying attention. It's only through really listening to others that you'll figure out how to help them. And if you can, speak up right then. Don't wait.

While Kevin thinks he's doing us all a favor, we're left with the perception that Kevin doesn't listen. Plus, while Kevin is listing all of the companies he can help with, everyone else has forgotten the companies Kevin needs help with (because sometimes we all have a little ADD!). Kevin leaves the room not only being perceived as a bad listener, but he also doesn't get any help from the group.

Give others an opportunity and a reason to help you. Pay attention. Listen carefully. And be worthy.

Be Relevant to Your Friends and Family

Being in a job search 24/7 is no picnic. And it's not for the people around you either. While you think you're doing them a favor by being singularly focused on finding that perfect opportunity, you're missing the bigger picture. Jobs come and go. But your friends and family will always be with you. Nobody likes the person who works all of the time. And nobody likes the person who job searches all of the time. Take advantage of the time you're given to spend quality time with your friends and family. Don't be the Debbie Downer that can only have fun after you find a job. Maybe in finding time to have fun, you'll end up meeting someone who leads you to a job.

Be Relevant to Your Faith

About a year into my search, my mom invited me to a Bible class. I told her I had no intention of hanging out with a bunch of Bible thumpers. But, as she so accurately pointed out, I had nothing else to do. Guilty as charged, I met her at the Bible class the following day. For the next two hours, I was on the edge of my seat – mesmerized by the teacher. Kevin Saunders was part historian, part geographer, part religion teacher and part comedian. Who knew the Bible could be so fascinating?!

This class (www.arizonabibleclass.com) gave me something to look forward to every Wednesday. It was through studying the Book of Job that I quit questioning God for all that I was going through. And I started embracing the idea that there really was a bigger plan. A bigger picture. A greater meaning to all of this. And while I couldn't see it at the time, I knew God had the plan all mapped out. And it was going to be a great plan! It had to be, right? For all I went through, it had to be one grand plan.

Seven years later, I ended up finishing the entire Bible and graduated from the class. Looking back, had I not been in a job search with lots of free time, I would have never taken the time to go through this class. As I look back at all of the things I've accomplished both work-wise and personally, this stands alone as number one. It gave me knowledge, but more importantly, it gave me strength. Strength to know that there's a bigger plan for me.

How's the plan working out so far? Pretty great!

If someone told me ten years ago that one day I'd be writing a book on job search, I never would have believed it. If someone told me I'd build a company that helps people in the job search, I never would have believed it. If someone told me I'd have to go through years of tough times in order to be the person I'm supposed to be, I would've said, "You've got the wrong Molly Wendell!"

But, it turns out, that's just what happened. And looking back, it appears that's what's supposed to have happened. I didn't know it at the time. And I wouldn't change it for the world.

In Closing

Take the time to be relevant. Take the time to figure out who you're supposed to be. And be the best person you can possibly be. Don't worry that all of the pieces don't seem to be fitting together like you planned. Sometimes life isn't about what's given to you, it's about what you make of it. Sometimes you have to go through some challenges to come out stronger on the other side. Sometimes you have to experience things to be more helpful to others.

What do you have to learn out of all of this? Take some moments to reflect and appreciate the gift of time you've been given. Maybe in not thinking about your job search, you can actually gain greater insight as to the path you need to follow. Maybe that's why you were given the gift of time in the first place.

Molly Wendell

AFTERWORD: TAKING FLIGHT AND LANDING

Well, that's it. I hope you've found this book interesting and informative. Enough to walk away with perhaps a few new approaches and ideas to help you land your next position sooner.

Some of these approaches and ideas might not be for you. Some, you may not believe are necessary or that they'll even work. The bottom line is you have to figure out what's right for you. But, please be open to trying something new. After all, what's the worst thing that could happen? You could be exactly where you are today... looking for a job.

Another important thing to remember. There might be a reason you're in this search. Quit fighting it. Embrace it. Ask yourself what it is that you really want or need to do (or need to learn). Be open to the idea that you may not need a job so much as you simply need an income. Be open to the possibility that opportunities come in all different forms. And it's usually through conversations with others that the most intriguing ones surface.

With this open mind, you'll be amazed at the doors that open up – leading you down the right path.

And remember. Everyone wants to help you. They just may not know it yet.

– Molly Wendell

P.S. There is so much more to say. Be sure to visit my Blog for frequent updates: www.mollywendell.com.

163

Molly Wendell

BONUS: MOLLY'S TAKEAWAY CHECKLISTS

CHAPTER 1: DO YOU KNOW WHY YOU WERE PUT IN THIS JOB SEARCH?

1. Don't waste precious time on the Internet when you could be talking with a real live person.
2. Remember, a recruiter will beat down your door if you're the perfect person for the job.
3. Focus forward. You've had a negative experience. That doesn't mean you should become a negative person.
4. You're going to find a fantastic opportunity. It may take longer than you think. It may take more work than you think. But you'll get there. And one day, you just might look back on this time and realize that you've become a better person because of it.

CHAPTER 2: THE BASICS

1. Get a professional-looking business card that shows your name, business phone number, email, and three areas of interest/expertise.
2. Make sure the signature line in your email has the same contact info as your business card.
3. Master the handshake.
4. Don't ever find yourself without a pen and paper.

CHAPTER 3: WHAT ARE YOU SUPPOSED TO DO IN LIFE?

1. Identify your passion and how you can position yourself to profit from it.
2. Don't be afraid to fail. Edison conducted thousands of experiments before he got the light bulb right.

3. Perceived dead ends can often lead to the right doors opening.
4. Reassess your aptitudes to identify your strengths and decide what you really want to do.

CHAPTER 4: TARGETING YOUR MARKET

1. Prepare for your search by targeting your industry, company, and dream position – be specific.
2. Network and ask questions until you know enough to sound like an expert.
3. If you're willing to relocate, start with where you want to be.
4. Be like Solar Mike, and make your luck happen.

CHAPTER 5: THE RESUME

1. Use your resume to position yourself for the job you want – not the ones you've already had.
2. Make sure it's free of clutter and looks highly professional.
3. Send your resume as a PDF attached to a cover email.
4. Create a resume for each position for which you are applying.

CHAPTER 6: ELECTRONIC TOOLS

1. The position you're looking for probably won't be posted online.
2. Learn to use social networking tools judiciously.
3. Every company has some degree of turnover. Make sure when an opening comes up, they think of you.
4. Meeting face-to-face is the only way to learn if that perfect position even exists.

CHAPTER 7: WORKING WITH RECRUITERS

1. Don't shop for a recruiter. Get referrals to them, and build a relationship.
2. Recruiters typically go to their client's competition for talent. If you're in the job search you may already be out of the running.
3. If a recruiter contacts you, schedule a time to talk after they've sent you the details.
4. Don't spend a large percentage of your job search in an area that fills such a small percentage of the jobs.

CHAPTER 8: JOB SEARCH MEETINGS

1. Go to every job search meeting prepared to talk about your background, what makes you different and desired position.
2. Accept, record, and follow up on every contact and lead you get.
3. Don't forget your manners. A call or email to thank someone for a referral (even a dead end) opens the door a little wider for the future.
4. The more new connections you have in your network, the more solid and effective it becomes for your job search today.

CHAPTER 9: NETWORKING EVENTS

1. A networking event is not the same thing as a job search meeting.
2. Be prepared to lead the conversation. Talk about things other people are interested in and ask lots of good questions. Avoid conversation-killing questions.
3. Be prepared to collect information. Bring a pen and paper and if someone has a lead for you, get their

contact information so you have control and you can follow up with them.

4. This is your chance to shine. Dress appropriately. Don't be boring or negative.

CHAPTER 10: GETTING A MEETING

1. Referrals are always better than introductions because you have more control.
2. Meet with people in person rather than over the phone or email.
3. Avoid the common pitfalls. Be low maintenance. Communicate clearly. Be professional, but not too formal.
4. Follow up diligently on every lead but be patient, even if it seems like dog years have gone by.

CHAPTER 11: THE INTERVIEW

1. Do your homework. Get all the background information you need to help you really know what's going on with the company and the decision makers.
2. Show up prepared to hold up your end of the interview process. Have your questions ready.
3. Have a smart answer ready for any stupid questions. Then don't let them ask any more questions. The interview isn't about you. Focus on them, their needs, expectations, plans for the future.
4. Learn their time line to fill the position and then follow up in a relevant way.

INDEX